Defeating the U-boat

Inventing Antisubmarine Warfare

The author thanks the Smith Richardson Foundation for its support, which helped make writing this story possible.

Contents

Foreword, *by Carnes Lord*   v

Introduction: "We Are Losing the War"   1

CHAPTER ONE   "The Submarine Boat Does Not and
                   Cannot Revolutionize
                   Naval Warfare"   5

CHAPTER TWO   Cutting the Thin Thread   25

CHAPTER THREE   "The Old Theories Have Been Tried and
                   Found Wanting"   47

CHAPTER FOUR   "We Run a Great Risk of Losing
                   the War"   57

Conclusion   69

Abbreviations   81

About the Author   83

The Newport Papers   85

Foreword

The emergence of operationally effective submarines in the decade or so preceding the outbreak of World War I revolutionized naval warfare. The pace of change in naval technologies generally in the late nineteenth century was unprecedented, but the submarine represented a true revolution in the nature of war at sea, comparable only to the emergence of naval aviation in the period following the First World War or of ballistic missiles and the atomic bomb following the Second. It is therefore not altogether surprising that the full promise and threat of this novel weapon were not immediately apparent to observers at the time. Even after submarines had proved their effectiveness in the early months of the war, navies were slow to react to the new strategic and operational environment created by them. The Royal Navy in particular failed to foresee the vulnerability of British maritime commerce to the German U-boat, especially after the Germans determined on a campaign of unrestricted submarine warfare—attack without warning on neutral as well as enemy merchant shipping—in 1917.

In *Defeating the U-boat: Inventing Antisubmarine Warfare*, Newport Paper 36, Jan S. Breemer tells the story of the British response to the German submarine threat. His account of Germany's "asymmetric" challenge (to use the contemporary term) to Britain's naval mastery holds important lessons for the United States today, the U.S. Navy in particular. The Royal Navy's obstinate refusal to consider seriously the option of convoying merchant vessels, which turned out to be the key to the solution of the U-boat problem, demonstrates the extent to which professional military cultures can thwart technical and operational innovation even in circumstances of existential threat. Although historical controversy continues to cloud this issue, Breemer concludes that the convoying option was embraced by the Royal Navy only under the pressure of civilian authority. Breemer ends his lively and informative study with some general reflections on military innovation and the requirements for fostering it.

CARNES LORD
Director, Naval War College Press
Newport, Rhode Island

"We Are Losing the War"

On 10 April 1917, Rear Admiral William Sowden Sims, U.S. Navy, sat across from the Royal Navy's Admiral of the Fleet Sir John Rushworth Jellicoe. Sims and his aide had arrived in London on that same day, less than twenty-four hours after their passenger steamer had docked in Liverpool. While they were at sea, on 6 April, the American Congress had declared war on Germany and its allies. Anticipating hostilities, the U.S. Navy Secretary, Josephus Daniels, had ordered Sims to London to, in Sims's words, "get in touch with the British Admiralty, to study the naval situation and learn how we could best and most quickly cooperate in the naval war."[1] Now, sitting across from him—"calm, smiling and imperturbable"—was the First Sea Lord. With operational responsibility for the entire British navy, Jellicoe was well placed to confirm the belief of Sims and most Americans that the British fleet "had the situation well in hand."[2]

It did not. Sims was shocked to learn that the struggle against the U-boats had been far less successful than was being portrayed in the American and British newspapers. When he realized that the numbers of sinkings of British and neutral merchantmen were three and four times larger than reported, Sims observed, "It looks as though the Germans were winning the war."[3] Jellicoe agreed. New, promising weapons, notably the depth charge, were being developed, but if the U-boats kept up their current pace of sinkings, they would not be ready in time. That was why it was critical that the U.S. Navy immediately send help in the way of destroyers and other small vessels. After his meeting, Sims cabled Washington that, "briefly stated, I consider that at the present moment we are losing the war."[4] He also warned Secretary Daniels that reports of British tactical successes against the U-boats should be treated with a great deal of skepticism. He wrote: "Accept *no* reports of submarine losses as authentic and certain unless survivors are captured or the submarine itself definitely located by dragging."[5] The April report on monthly ship losses seemed to bear out Sims's fear. In what would turn out to be the peak month of the U-boats' productivity, 860,334 tons of shipping were sunk. Also, the exchange rate between the numbers of allied ships lost and U-boats sunk was, from the defender's perspective, the worst ever—167 : 1.[6]

Seventeen months later, in what historian Paul Halpern has called a "curiously anticlimactic" occasion, the German submarine fleet surrendered. Between 20 November and 1 December 1918, 114 U-boats gave themselves up in British ports; more were seized in German harbors.[7] In October, the last full month of the war, shipping losses had declined to 116,237 tons.[8] As a result of this happy turn of events, wrote one British army officer, he and his fellow officers at the allied headquarters in France lacked only "certain material—particularly . . . chocolate, biscuits, and tinned fruits in the canteens."[9]

How had the desperate situation Sims was told about in the spring of 1917 come to pass? How was it possible that a craft that had shown its seaworthiness only two decades before and that, right up to the war, was still being dismissed by many naval officers as more dangerous to its own crew than its intended victim had managed effectively to neutralize the most powerful fleet in the world? When it did, the submarine overturned one of the most sacred tenets of the prevailing conception of sea power— the notion, expressed most cogently only a few years before by Alfred Thayer Mahan, that sea power was about command of the sea, that its possession turned on victory in decisive battles between fleets of dreadnoughts. According to this dogma, the side that won command accomplished two things simultaneously thereby. First, "owning" command meant that the opponent could no longer use the sea for its purposes—for instance, to ship goods and raw materials or threaten seaborne landings. Next, the side in command had the unfettered use of the sea for *its* own purposes—moving supplies and troops, launching attacks against the enemy shore, and so forth. The tonnage war waged by the U-boats revolutionized naval warfare by rendering obsolete this basic principle of pre–World War I naval thinking. The transformation of naval warfare from the surface of the seas to the water column below had served to bifurcate command of the sea. Britain in 1917 still controlled the seas in, as Sims put it, the "old Nelsonian sense"—its Grand Fleet of dreadnoughts kept its German counterpart, the High Sea Fleet, in port, and the German merchant fleet had effectively disappeared from the oceans.[10] But that same Grand Fleet could not guarantee the safety of Britain's own trade routes and ensure the arrival of enough foodstuffs, war supplies, and so on.

In the end, of course, the British and their allies did manage to defeat the U-boat's strategic goal of economic strangulation. The U-boats' defeat at the *strategic* level of war bears emphasizing, because it can be argued with considerable force that the allies never quite managed to defeat the German submarine fleet tactically or technically. True, U-boat losses in absolute terms went up very significantly in 1917 and 1918, from twenty-two in 1916 to sixty-three and sixty-nine in 1917 and 1918, respectively. Much of this was due to the introduction of the depth charge and better mines. But these gains become less significant when it is realized that thanks to new construction, the overall size of the U-boat threat remained fairly constant.[11] Moreover, it stands to reason that the probability of a U-boat being detected and attacked successfully went up as more and more U-boats went to sea.

Countering the submarine's revolutionary impact on the old command-of-the-sea principle and restoring the ability to use the seas at acceptable cost called for equally revolutionary countermeasures. Those countermeasures had little to do with new weapons or technologies. Both did play a role, of course, notably the depth charge and hydro-acoustic devices. But these and other technological innovations made collectively a comparatively small contribution to the *conceptual* counterrevolution that was at the heart of the U-boat's final defeat in World War I. That defeat was made possible, first and foremost, by compromising what was arguably the very ethos of the naval profession, namely the belief that wars at sea are fought and won by aggressively seeking out and sinking the enemy.

Notes

1. Rear Adm. William Sowden Sims, *The Victory at Sea* (Garden City, N.Y.: Doubleday, Page, 1921), p. 3.

2. Ibid., p. 7.

3. Ibid., p. 9. Also, Admiral of the Fleet, the Rt. Hon. Earl Jellicoe, *The Submarine Peril: Admiralty Policy in 1917* (London: Cassell, 1934), pp. 70–71.

4. Sims, *Victory at Sea*, p. 43.

5. Sims to Daniels, 19 April 1917, in *Anglo-American Naval Relations 1917–1919*, ed. Michael Simpson (Aldershot, U.K.: Gower for the Navy Records Society, 1991), p. 42 [emphasis in the original].

6. Paul G. Halpern, *A Naval History of World War I* (Annapolis, Md.: Naval Institute Press, 1994), p. 341.

7. Ibid., p. 448.

8. Ibid., p. 423.

9. "G.S.O.," *G.H.Q. (Montreuil-sur-Mer)* (London: Philip Allan, 1920), pp. 130–31.

10. Sims, *Victory at Sea*, p. 21.

11. The total number of U-boats on 1 January 1916 stood at 133; on 1 January 1917, 142; and on 11 November 1918, 134. Two hundred twenty-nine more boats were under construction at the time of the armistice.

CHAPTER ONE

"The Submarine Boat Does Not and Cannot Revolutionize Naval Warfare"

The submarine was history's first "absolute weapon."[1] It was so because never before had a weapon been created that so defied man's scientific ability to produce quickly a counterweapon. For one, the submarine was the first man-made weapon to go about its war-making business in the third dimension. This produced an unprecedented challenge for the development of countermeasures. Previously, striking a target with some sort of projectile had required a fire-control solution in only one or two dimensions. One-dimensional targets—for example, land-based fortifications—are easiest to hit, because they are fixed. Two-dimensional, or moving, targets present a much more difficult gunnery problem. During the age of sail, the problem was "solved" by engaging at point-blank ranges, making the target nearly immobile relative to the gun. The industrial revolution at sea during the second half of the nineteenth century had made this impossible, however. Fighting ranges had, by the time the submarine appeared on the scene, expanded to thousands of yards, and the problem of hitting a moving ship from a platform that itself is moving was barely beginning to be solved. The submarine's ability to navigate not only on a plane but also up and down presented an even more complex fire-control problem—even for a visible target.

The submarine's invisibility—at least some of the time—and its ability therefore to move and attack unseen posed an unprecedented problem for the traditional tools of naval power. In fact, there were two problems. First, how does a ship moving on the surface of the oceans defend itself against attack "below the belt"? Second, if it survives, how does it find and sink the unseen attacker? These were questions that particularly concerned the British naval leadership. For years, their lordships had been wont to ignore or dismiss as wasteful tinkering the underwater designs of inventors all over the world. Even as the early experimental craft slowly matured and demonstrated a real ability to maneuver underwater, it did not make sense for the country that had by far the world's largest investment in "legacy" seagoing forces to encourage a weapon that might undermine that investment. Two developments forced the Royal Navy to reverse course and acknowledge that the "submarine torpedo-boat" had passed beyond the experimental stage and that, like it or not, the service would likely have to contend with it in future wars.

The first development was the growing underwater fleet of Britain's traditional enemy at sea, the French navy. The French had been experimenting with *sous-marins* since the 1860s. They established the world's first submarine branch in 1888, when the thirty-ton *Gymnote* was commissioned. Five years later, the much larger (266 tons) *Gustave Zédé* (named after *Gymnote*'s designer) was launched, and two others *(Narval* and *Morse)* were completed before the turn of the century. In 1899 the French staged a series of highly publicized exercises in which *Zédé* repeatedly and successfully "attacked" the battleship *Magenta.* One observer's account related how the submarine accomplished the "extraordinary exploit of sending a torpedo in an absolutely straight line between the funnels of the battle-ship."[2] Frenchmen and Britons alike had no doubt about the event's significance, coming as it did on the heels of the Anglo-French crisis at Fashoda. In France, a public subscription organized by the newspaper *Le Matin* collected more than a million francs, enough to buy two more submarines.[3] One rumor even had it that France planned to build no fewer than a hundred of the underwater vessels.[4] Britain as yet had none.

The other development occurred on the opposite side of the Atlantic. In 1899 the U.S. Navy's chief engineer, John Lowe, announced that he was entirely satisfied with the recently completed trials of a seventy-five-ton submarine *(Holland VI)* built by John P. Holland. The craft had proved, he said, that it was capable of making "a veritable attack upon the enemy unseen and undetectable, and that therefore, she is an engine of warfare of terrible potency which the government must necessarily adopt into its service."[5] Although the American navy ordered only five more Holland types instead of the fifty Lowe had urged, the message was loud and clear at Whitehall: the submarine could no longer be dismissed as little more than France's latest attempt to solve its navy's hopeless inferiority by way of a theoretically brilliant but practically useless "quick fix." The American submarine buy had changed things altogether. In a note written to the Royal Navy's future First Sea Lord, Sir John "Jackie" Fisher, one rear admiral admitted that he did not know whether submarines would or would not be useful in warfare. But, he thought, considering the fact that a "common-sense level-headed nation like that of the United States, has tried and adopted them, it would appear probable that such craft must have some value in warlike operations."[6]

The corollary was, of course, that if the submarine was going to be a practical engine of war, the British fleet had better learn how to defend against it. The head of the service had no difficulty identifying the crux of the defensive problem to come: first, "How to find them," and next, "How to destroy them."[7] Five improved Holland types, to be built in Britain under license from the Electric Boat company, were ordered from the United States to start the navy's education in underwater warfare.

After having studiously ignored the submarine for years, Britain's naval leadership could hardly admit that the French might have been on the right path all along, that they were suddenly persuaded that the craft might usefully complement the "real" fleet. The purchase of the Holland vessels was officially justified as having chiefly "experimental purposes."[8] It was patently obvious that the problem of finding and destroying an enemy submarine could not be solved by another submarine. Very limited research toward solving the first half of the antisubmarine warfare (ASW) problem—detecting the submarine—had begun in the early 1890s and had focused on developing a practical hydrophone. However, little progress was made during the next couple of decades; when war broke out, only a handful of ships had been fitted with a mix of British- and U.S.-made systems. Under favorable conditions—a calm sea with little wind, and with engines stopped—it was sometimes possible actually to hear a noisy U-boat. But these were rare occasions, and in any case, the early devices were omnidirectional systems: they could not tell from which direction the noise came.[9]

As far as destroying the submarine was concerned, efforts during the prewar years were concentrated, naturally enough, on developing some sort of underwater explosive. Basically, two different types of ordnance were needed. The first was a mine to protect ports and harbors against an enemy submarine blockade and, on the offensive side, barricade the enemy's submarine bases. Next needed was some sort of ship-carried explosive for use against submarines caught at sea. Sea mines were already familiar weapons of war; many countries, including Great Britain, relied on (shore controlled) minefields to protect ports and harbors. In Britain, as in the United States, the "static" defense of the coast with guns and minefields was the army's responsibility, the navy being left free to pursue would-be invaders on the high seas. This burden sharing fully reflected the Royal Navy's self-image as a "blue water" force: it existed to seek out the enemy wherever he might be, not to tie itself to coastal waters and wait for the enemy to show up. This offensive ethos had difficulty accommodating mines. They were seen as defensive weapons, the "asymmetric"—and rather unsporting—resort of the weaker power. It is no surprise then that the technical development of mines and mine countermeasures did not figure prominently among the Royal Navy's pre–World War I priorities.[10] In 1894, and again in 1903, the Admiralty canceled all development of independent mines for use other than harbor defense.[11] Programs were resumed after the Russo-Japanese War, but years of official vacillation saddled Britain with a stockpile of weapons that were notoriously unreliable and designed to sink surface ships, not submarines.

Equally poorly developed in 1914 were means for attacking and sinking submerged submarines. Two weapons were in the inventory when the war began: explosive sweeps and the so-called lance-bomb. The first, which came in several versions, basically involved a ship-towed hydroplane carrying a guncotton charge. The idea was to cross a suspected U-boat's track, entangle it in some part of the cable, and then electrically detonate the charge.[12] Most naval officers on the eve of war expected little from the device, but the alternative, the lance-bomb, was even less palatable. This was a hand-thrown weapon, consisting of a seven-pound charge attached to a wooden handle between three and four and a half feet long. Supposedly, a strong man could throw the weapon seventy-five yards.[13] The fact that some twenty thousand of the devices were produced during the war, even though any analysis could have easily foretold that they almost certainly presented a greater danger to the "launch platforms" than intended victims, is a clue to the desperate state of ASW at the time. Admiral Fisher told Prime Minister Asquith as much in a memorandum less than four months before war broke out: "No word of a submarine destroyer has ever been heard because it has been forced upon us, by experience, that submarines cannot fight submarines, nor has any success-ful antidote been found even by the most bitter antisubmarine experts with unlimited means for experiments."[14]

"The Question of the Protection of British Maritime Commerce Is Not an Important One"

In his autobiography, which appeared a year after World War I had ended, Admiral Sir Percy Scott—the "father" of modern Royal Navy gunnery—reported that the depth charge could have been developed and in use in 1914, two years before the first models actually entered the fleet.[15] He blamed the Admiralty's lack of interest in the submarine and, hence, submarine defenses.[16] It is probably fairer to say that the problem had less to do with a lack of interest per se than a failure to appreciate fully how much the sub-marine and its capabilities had changed since the first flotillas were formed ten or so years earlier. Intimately related was the failure to reconsider seriously how the enemy might use these much more advanced capabilities. Although it was well known on the eve of World War I that the submarine of 1914 was capable of venturing much farther out to sea than its first-generation predecessor, it was still expected to busy itself mainly with defense against a would-be blockading fleet and in surreptitious, long-range scouting. Radio had improved considerably, and it was thought that forward-deployed submarines could give early warning of enemy fleet movements. Ironically, the subma-rine soon became the surveillance platform of choice, in part because by 1914, its at-sea endurance was better than that of most destroyers.

Most important, neither side—Britain or Germany—had given but the most fleeting thought to the possibility that the submarine might be used against other than "legitimate"—that is, naval—targets, that its victims might be civilian shipping instead. It was not that the idea of attacking the opponent's seaborne commerce itself was unimaginable; commerce raiding had been practiced for centuries, and British naval planners fully anticipated having to deal with it again in the next war. It was the submarine's *method* that made its use as a commerce raider unthinkable for most naval officers. Namely, it was patently obvious that the craft's diminutive size and small crew effectively prevented it from engaging in antitonnage warfare in conformance with the internationally agreed Prize Regulations. Sinking merchantmen without warning and without ensuring the safety of passengers and crew was simply "not done" by civilized nations.[17] Winston Churchill, then the Admiralty's First Lord (roughly the equivalent of minister of the navy), fairly summed up this attitude in a memo to Admiral Fisher, after the latter had written that Germany would likely use its submarines in exactly this manner. Churchill thought his senior naval officer had written an "excellent" paper but that it was "to some extent, marred by the prominence" it gave to the idea of a U-boat commerce war. "I do not believe," he wrote, "this would ever be done by a civilized power." To emphasize his abhorrence, he suggested that a German decision to go ahead anyway would justify brutal retaliatory measures, such as spreading pestilence, poisoning the water of the perpetrator's great cities, and assassinating its leaders.[18] Interestingly, in what seems to be a case of wishful thinking, some naval officers thought that the submarine's very inability to abide by the Prize Regulations meant that it could not and would not pose a threat to commerce.[19]

The rejection of the idea that a civilized power would destroy private property on the high seas without warning was certainly understandable; the concept of "total war" between *nations,* not just armies, had yet to be born. But this alone cannot explain Britain's dismal lack of preparedness. The fact of the matter is that the Royal Navy saw the protection of commerce, be it against raiders on the surface of the sea or underneath, as an unglamorous, secondary, and worst of all, *defensive* priority that could not be allowed to interfere with what the service considered its primary responsibility: to seek out and battle the enemy's fleet. An Admiralty note in 1905 said it as follows: "The first duty of British fleets and squadrons will be to seek out the corresponding fleets and squadrons of the enemy with a view to bringing them to action and fighting for that which is the only really decisive factor—the command of the sea."[20]

The Admiralty reluctantly acknowledged its responsibility for the safe arrival of overseas foodstuffs but made patently clear that it would brook no political interference in its war preparations. A royal commission charged with looking into the wartime vulnerability of the country's supply line was told that the navy would not sanction any defensive scheme that it believed would weaken the fleet's readiness to fight the big bat-tle. The pertinent paragraph in the commission's final report is revealing:

> In commenting upon the apprehension that the disposition of the British Fleet, squadrons, or ships might be adversely affected and the free action of the Admiralty impaired by popular pressure, exer-cised through Parliament upon the Government, thus influencing the Admiralty instructions to the admirals, it was remarked that the Admiralty could never allow their action to be influenced by any pressure, and yet consent to remain responsible for the conduct of the war.[21]

The Royal Navy's war plans of this period, as well as its estimate of Germany's plans at sea, faithfully reflected its preoccupation with the big-battle idea and the cavalier dis-missal of the possible danger to trade. Its "War Plans and Distribution of the Fleet" of 1907–1908 estimated that attacks on British commerce had the lowest priority in the German scheme for war at sea. The Germans were expected to aim, like the British themselves, at a decisive clash between battle fleets.[22] Consequently, enemy attacks against trade would be, according to the plan's authors, the "least serious of all the pos-sible German operations of war." Even if, contrary to expectations, the enemy attempted a concerted raiding campaign, superior British naval power would "effec-tively prevent any organized attack on our trade" and reduce it to "simple pinpricks." The British navy, the plans continued, really had only two worries: first, to bring the German fleet to decisive action; and second, to "resist the pressure of public opinion and refuse to be coerced into departing from its carefully considered war plan" just because a handful of merchantmen had been taken by enemy raiders.[23]

What makes this attitude particularly striking is that the few studies that had been done on the subject had suggested that German raiders might have considerable success, at least in the early part of a war. For example, in a memorandum less than three months before the outbreak of war, the director of the Admiralty's Trade Division, Captain Richard Webb, estimated that Britain's "foreign-going" merchant fleet could lose as many as seventy-seven ships per week. The memorandum did not explain how this number had been arrived at but claimed it could be achieved by no more than four cruisers and twelve armed liners in the Atlantic and a smattering of commerce raiders elsewhere.[24] (In the event, the U-boats did not achieve such a high kill rate even at the height of the unrestricted campaign.)

The Webb memorandum did not mention submarines; neither did the Admiralty's war plans of 1907–1908. This is perhaps understandable, since the first U-boat *(U-1)* was not commissioned until late 1906—that is, about the time the plans were being com-pleted. Could it therefore be said that the Navy's seemingly casual attitude toward the protection of commerce reflected, in fact, a balanced and realistic assessment of the threat at the time? Or putting it in a different way, if the German navy of 1906 had owned the two dozen or so submarines it possessed at the start of World War I, would the Royal Navy's treatment of the threat have been different? Indeed, planners began to pay more than passing attention to Germany's nascent underwater fleet in 1909–10, when about half a dozen boats had been commissioned. But the addition of this novel enemy capability seems to have had little impact on the plans of 1907–1908. True, it had become broadly agreed that once Germany had acquired a sizable underwater fleet, the Royal Navy might need some time to exercise its command of the "narrow seas" (the Channel, its approaches, and the seas surrounding Great Britain) by the time-honored means of battle-fleet "sweeps." The First Sea Lord, Admiral Fisher, in particular warned that swarms of U-boats might make the narrow seas quite untenable by conventional warships. One of his publicists, retired army colonel Charles à Court Repington, "leaked" Fisher's views in a series of journal articles in 1910 concluding that "there will be no place for any great ship in the North Sea."[25] With what turned out to be a surprising prescience, he painted a submarine antitonnage campaign that would undermine the nation's ability to feed "some tens of millions," would cause a great rise in food and fuel prices, and very possibly provoke food riots. Since nothing had been invented or built to defeat the U-boat, he wrote, "nothing we can effect with naval means can, with any certainty, prevent German submarines from putting to sea when they please, and from appearing off our coasts at their own sweet will."[26]

Few among the British naval leadership, though, subscribed to Fisher and Repington's bleak prognosis. Most appear to have shared (then) Rear Admiral Jellicoe's view instead. It basically held that the U-boat would almost certainly make the planning and execution of a decisive fleet-against-fleet battle much more complicated but that with enough energy and effort, the problem would be brought under control and the North Sea made safe for a modern-day Trafalgar. In a note in 1909, Jellicoe wrote that even with a maximum effort, it would be another eight years before Germany had enough submarines truly to menace the North Sea. In the event, the fleet might at some point have to be kept out of harm's way but, over time, enough U-boats would be sunk to allow the big ships to come out and fight a decisive action.[27] Jellicoe did not make clear how his navy would go about eradicating the U-boats.

Ironically, the British estimate of the German naval threat was not much off the mark. The German naval leadership, by and large, shared the "acknowledged axiom, proven from war-history, that the struggle at sea must be directed to gaining the mastery of the sea, i.e., to removing all opposition which stands in the way of its free and unhindered use."[28] The alternative—guerilla warfare against the enemy's commerce—was regarded by most German naval officers as a winless proposition. That said, the idea of using submarines to attack commerce was certainly known and discussed in professional journals.[29] According to Germany's official account of the war at sea, the U-boat arm's younger officers—who were more familiar than their battle-fleet colleagues with the new diesel boats' capabilities—were especially enthusiastic proponents.[30] There is no evidence, however, that any formal planning on these lines took place before the war.[31] Instead, prewar planning for the U-boat flotillas was focused mainly on how they could best be used to create favorable conditions for a decisive fleet battle. In particular, the U-boats were seen as the key to whittling down the numerically superior Grand Fleet to approximate parity *(Kräfteausgleich)* with Germany's High Sea Fleet. Then, and only then, would the Kaiser's dreadnoughts sally forth and engage their opposite numbers. The only problem was that the British had come to the same conclusion: that the narrow seas would likely be a submarine and mine trap. The U-boats would soon take their toll among patrolling cruisers and destroyers, but the prize targets, the Grand Fleet's battleships and battle cruisers, would keep their distance, in northernmost Scotland.

If neither British nor German prewar planning anticipated a submarine tonnage war, can it yet be argued that there were enough "indicators and warnings" to make this in fact a plausible contingency against which Britain's Admiralty planners *should* have guarded? A reasonable case can be made that the basic conceptual and material "building blocks" for this kind of warfare were already there, that the unrestricted U-boat campaign of 1917–18 was far more conceivable in 1914 than planners on either side of the North Sea were willing to admit at the time. To begin with, the idea, so repulsive to Churchill, that a "civilized" opponent would sink a nonmilitary vessel, including crew and cargo, without giving proper warning and allowing the crew time to abandon ship was hardly without precedent. Its progenitor can be found in the "Jeune École." This school of naval strategic thought, which, though centered in France, had adherents among naval officers throughout the Continent, argued that "mosquito fleets" of torpedo boats and gunboats, not big-gun armorclads, were the weapons of future war at sea; that rather than seeking battle à la Trafalgar, the aim should be to destroy the enemy's oceanic trade, attack his port cities at night, and thus trigger financial panic and "bread riots" among the working class.[32] Among the movement's leading lights were French admiral Hyacinthe-Laurent-Théophile Aube and his journalist protégé Gabriel Charmes. Writing in 1886, Charmes urged France's navy to reequip itself for *guerre de course* fought with "microbes." Small and seemingly insignificant flotillas of torpedo boats and gunboats would, under the cover of darkness, ambush and destroy the largest unarmed liners afloat.[33] Aube made clear that unlike in the past, ships, their crews, and cargoes would not be captured but sunk without warning: "Having followed the liner from afar, come nightfall, the torpedo-boat will, perfectly silently and quietly send the liner, its cargo, crew, and passengers to the abyss. His soul not only at ease but fully satisfied, the captain of the torpedo-boat will continue his cruise."[34]

Naval historian Theodore Ropp has written that despite superficial similarities, there was a vast difference between the Jeune École's idea of commerce warfare and the German practice in 1917–18. The French idea, he wrote, was to panic the British into ceasing hostilities; the German plan, on the other hand, was literally to starve the opponent into submission.[35] The distinction is a fair, albeit subtle, one, but other than that, the Aube-Charmes scheme was no more humane or in closer accord with traditional prize-taking rules than the U-boats' unrestricted "blockade" thirty years later. Raoul Castex, one of the most innovative French naval strategic thinkers of the inter–world war years, certainly thought that his country, not the Germans, could and should take credit for inventing the idea of unrestricted commerce warfare. Clearly, he wrote, in 1920, "the theory of commerce warfare with torpedoes was not exactly born on the other side of the Rhine. The Germans, as so often, no more than appropriated the invention of others."

The Jeune École's vision of unrestricted commerce warfare came to naught, in part, when exercises showed that the small (fifty ton) craft that Aube and Charmes envisaged as the scourges of the seas were simply not up to the task. Wear and tear on men and matériel made extended operations impossible. True, the turn-of-the-century submarine was, if anything, even less qualified to "keep the sea." Machinery and weapons frequently broke down (the colocation of gasoline engines and unshielded electrical wiring did not help), the craft was blind when submerged (functional periscopes did not appear until after 1904), and together these two limitations made the vessel highly accident-prone. Matters were very different, however, on the eve of World War I: between 1904 and 1914 the submarine had become a reliable and seaworthy navigational and weapons-carrying platform. This is not a *post facto* assessment—in exercise after exercise during the immediate prewar years, "lessons learned" by naval professionals on both sides of the North Sea highlighted the submarine's growing high-seas range and stamina. It is useful to summarize the submarine's technical progress during the decade leading up to World War I.

The typical submarine of 1904 displaced about 150 tons; its successor ten years later was five times larger. Greater hull volume allowed larger, more powerful engines and batteries, so that speed nearly doubled—from less than ten knots to about seventeen knots on the surface, and from five to ten knots submerged. Even more impressive were improvements in range and endurance. Thanks to the introduction of the diesel engine and increases in bunker capacity, the surface cruising range of the typical submarine had expanded from 1,000 to 1,500 nautical miles in 1904 to 7,500 nautical miles or more by 1914. When war broke out, design bureaus on both sides had plans for truly oceangoing boats, with cruising ranges of some ten thousand nautical miles. It also bears mentioning in this connection that the submarine of 1914 exhibited a design philosophy that was very different from that of its progenitor. Most of the early boats had conical hull forms. This was fine as long as the boat was underwater, but on the surface it made for an extremely unstable platform. The submarine of 1914 had a very different hull shape, for by that time professional design and operational opinion had firmly come out in favor of the much more shiplike, "submersible" submarine. It was double hulled, with a cylindrical inner hull containing the crew, machinery, and stores, and a free-flooding outer hull providing stability for surface cruising. This shift not only produced a far more stable platform but improved surface speeds and made the vessel much stronger. The double-hulled, diesel-electric submersible would dominate undersea warfare until the introduction of the nuclear-driven submarine in the 1950s.

The submersible spent most of the time on the surface, where it was theoretically more susceptible to detection. Practically though, the risk was small. Exercises had repeatedly demonstrated that a submarine in an awash condition—with only the conning tower out of the water—was extremely difficult to spot. Usually, the submarine made the "first detection" in plenty of time to disappear below the waves. Nevertheless, partly as the result of a series of disastrous collisions with surface ships, much was done prior to the outbreak of World War I to speed up the process of submerging. Some of the early boats needed as much as fifteen minutes, but by 1914 a diving time of five minutes or less had become standard for a boat when fully surfaced, about one minute from an awash condition. When submerged, the average submarine of 1904 could navigate at a depth of about thirty-five meters; ten years later, fifty meters was common. Even before the war started, the technology was in hand to operate at the much greater depths that became the practice by 1917. However, until the invention of the depth charge, there was no obvious need for doing so.

The submarine's armament had become more lethal also. Despite its comparatively high cost and indifferent performance during the Russo-Japanese War of 1904–1905, the torpedo had become firmly established as the boat's principal weapon system. The typical torpedo of 1914 was, like its predecessor of 1904, a "straight-runner," with preset guidance provided by a gyroscope. The weight of the warhead on the 1914 torpedo too was not much different from the 1904 model—about two hundred pounds; a contact fuse was still the only means of triggering the device. Important improvements had come in speed and striking range. Whereas the "old" torpedoes boasted a (range dependent) speed of up to twenty knots, the 1914 types attained speeds up to thirty knots and greater.[36] Advertised ranges were up to 2,500 yards, but *effective* ranges were closer to some five hundred yards for the typical 1904 model and two thousand for its 1914 successor.[37] Even more important for the submarine's maturation as a high-seas fighting platform was its much improved weapons payload. The average submarine in 1904 carried two or three torpedoes; six was the norm in 1914.

One important drawback of the torpedo was cost: a single torpedo built in 1914 cost about a thousand British pounds sterling.[38] This does not sound excessive until it is realized that this equates to roughly $100,000 today. For this reason, virtually all submarines on the eve of war carried a deck-mounted gun, typically with a caliber of three-plus inches. The U-boats were unique in the sense that they were the only submarines armed with high-elevation guns to fight off aircraft. One other improvement that took place between 1904 and 1914 in the submarine's capability as weapon carrier was in the area of mine warfare. The Russians were the first to build a dedicated minelaying submarine, when they laid the keel for *Krab* in 1908.[39] After war broke out, the British and Germans followed suit and adapted their submarines for minelaying tasks, first by using the standard torpedo tubes but later by imitating the Russian example and building special-purpose boats fitted with vertical or angled mine "chutes." Depending on the size of the submarine, up to two dozen or so mines could be carried.

The evolution of the submarine from a near-shore, low-endurance defensive weapon to an oceangoing offensive platform coincided with the maturation of wireless for reliable long-distance communication. In 1904, shipboard radio was still a rarity; ten years later, all the major navies had installed sets on large surface combatants and submarines. To be sure, these devices still had a limited send-and-receive capability. They were low powered (half a kilowatt to about one kilowatt), which allowed communication in the medium-frequency band over a distance of some thirty to fifty nautical miles.[40] Very early in the war, however, the Germans found that their equipment was far better than they themselves had thought. In early 1915, reliable ship-to-shore communications up to 140 nautical miles were possible. Not long afterward, radio contact up to a thousand nautical miles was established, and by the middle of 1915 U-boats maintained regular communications with their headquarters in Wilhelmshaven from as far away as the Atlantic and Mediterranean.[41] Ironically, the very excellence of the U-boats' radio gear created an unexpected vulnerability, in that it encouraged crews to engage in what Patrick Beesly has called "unduly garrulous" behavior.[42] The result was that, starting in late 1914, the code breakers of the British Naval Intelligence Division's "Room 40" were able to supply a steady stream of strategic intelligence about the U-boat fleet's strength and general whereabouts.[43] This information was complemented in the spring of 1915 by "radio plots" that marked the location of individual U-boats. These plots were the product of a chain of radio-direction-finding stations that were erected along the coasts of England and Ireland. Fixes, based on the intersection of at least two radio bearings, were accurate to within a radius of twenty to fifty nautical miles.[44] This kind of information would prove extremely useful for the routing of convoys, but it rarely, if ever, was accurate or timely enough to bring about a successful tactical prosecution by a "hunter-killer" sloop or destroyer.

To summarize, the submarine of 1914 was clearly a far more formidable weapon than its forerunner at the turn of the century. It had evolved from a mechanically unreliable and slow coastal-defense platform that could stay at sea for only a few days with less than a handful of not-so-accurate weapons to a true oceangoing craft that could stay out for weeks and use a combination of mines, torpedoes, and gunfire to endanger shipping anywhere between midocean and home port. During the same period, and even though naval professionals on both sides of the impending conflict were acutely aware of the "modern" submarine's potential, nothing to speak of had been accomplished with respect to countermeasures. Later in the war, when the U-boats seemed frightfully close to their goal of economic strangulation, Britain's chief of naval staff lamely defended the prewar failure to innovate against the submarine by suggesting there had been no pressing need at the time. "It should be remembered," he said, "that the submarine was in its infancy at the outbreak of war."[45] The problem was that if the U-boat had been in 1914 in its "infancy," *antisubmarine* warfare had yet to be born.

"As for the U-boats, the Admiralty Says Little but Does Much"

When Britain declared war on Germany on 4 August 1914, the Royal Navy boasted the world's most numerous submarine fleet—seventy-seven boats.[46] France, with some sixty, took second place. Germany, by contrast, owned a grand total of only twenty-eight. Several were already obsolete, but the ten last-built boats *(U-19 through U-28)* were, without a doubt, superior to any foreign-built submarine. Sixteen additional U-boats were under construction, and additional orders were placed between August and November.[47] If the diminutive size of this force alone is not proof that Germany's naval planners were not then thinking in terms of a major war against commerce, the following may be: almost until the very day war was declared, Germany's largest U-boat yard, the Germaniawerft, was negotiating—with the approval of the naval staff—with the Greek government over the sale of five U-boats then on order for Germany's own navy.[48]

Limited numbers accounted for one reason why it took some time for the submarine's revolutionary impact on war to be registered. The other reason was that during the first six months of the war, Germany used the U-boats mostly according to the "old," prerevolutionary rules of sea warfare. That is to say, they were employed as "legitimate" weapons war against "legitimate" targets of war—the enemy's fleet. Since this was precisely what the British had expected all along, the results, though dramatic on occasion, fell far short of the German goal of creating a more even balance of dreadnought power. For one thing, the Grand Fleet gave the U-boats few opportunities to stalk and attack its battleships. The fleet retreated to its anchorage at Scapa Flow in northernmost Scotland, whence it made occasional sweeps into the North Sea. The daily routine of enforcing the distant blockade of Germany's ports and harbors was left to cruisers and destroyers. Many of these were older vessels, but even so they were usually faster than submarines and therefore difficult to approach for a favorable torpedo-firing position. Of course, the very fact that fear of mines and submarines had compelled the Royal Navy's battleships to vacate the narrow seas was itself an indication that the old Mahanian verity that command of the sea rested with the biggest ships had lost much of its meaning. The new asymmetric nature of war at sea became dramatically evident on 22 September 1914. On that day, a single submarine managed to sink, within one hour, three armored cruisers—*Aboukir, Cressy,* and *Hogue*—on routine patrol in the North Sea. More than 2,500 men died, more than at Trafalgar. Julian Corbett recalled after the war that "nothing that had yet occurred had so emphatically proclaimed the change that had come over naval warfare, and never perhaps had so great a result been obtained by means relatively so small."[49]

The disproportionate effect of the handful of U-boats in 1914 on the world's most powerful battle fleet showed in a warning from Jellicoe to his subordinate commanders that should the Grand and High Sea fleets meet for the much-desired decisive battle, the enemy might feign a tactical retreat with the objective of drawing the Grand Fleet into a mine or submarine trap.[50] In later battle orders, which were in force at Jutland, Jellicoe spelled out the operational and, for that matter, strategic implications of his concern: should the enemy "turn away" his line of battle, he wrote, "it may be expected that I shall not follow a decided turn of this nature . . . as I should anticipate that it is made for the purpose of taking us over submarines."[51]

The loss of *Aboukir, Cressy, Hogue,* and, a couple of weeks earlier, the cruiser *Pathfinder* evidently impressed the British more than the Germans. While the German naval leadership was pleased with this dramatic demonstration of the U-boat's war-fighting capabilities, it was also acutely aware that sinking older cruisers would not get it closer to *"der Tag"* with a roughly even balance of battle-fleet forces. If anything, the British cruiser losses had made the chances of a decisive battle on German terms even less likely, for the sinking of *Pathfinder* had caused Jellicoe to take the Grand Fleet to an even more distant anchorage on the northwest coast of Scotland.[52] In a memorandum of 28 December 1914, *Kapitän zur See* Zenker of the naval staff set forth the implications for Germany's naval strategy in general and the role of the U-boats in particular:

> It has been demonstrated that our submarines have not succeeded now for a long time in gaining any results worthy of note, despite the fact that they have been making cruises for a long time and have carried them out with great boldness. In the future prosecution of the war we will therefore be able to count neither on an equality of strength before the battle due to the use of our light forces nor on the opponent's changing his strategy as long as we continue ours unchanged.[53]

The question was this: If the British were unlikely to change their strategy, what changes could Germany make? In particular, how could the U-boats' surprising war-fighting potential be put to better use? The answer depended, in part, of course, on Germany's overall strategic goals at sea. If a modern-day Trafalgar was still the goal, Zenker's suggestion of closer tactical cooperation with the High Sea Fleet's battleships might be the solution. Zenker thought that a better strategy of reducing the Grand Fleet's numbers prior to a decisive battle might be to use the High Sea Fleet as bait and then trap the British in a forward screen of submarines. After these had taken their toll, the High Sea Fleet would be in a position to fight its battle on much more even terms.[54]

Zenker's scheme of using the U-boats in support of a decisive battle might have made some sense in the early days of the war, when it was popularly expected that the troops would be home by Christmas.[55] From the German perspective, this happy outcome was predicated on the rapid occurrence of at least *two* decisive battles—one on land that would break the back of the French army, and the other at sea against the British fleet. Come Christmas, though, it had become patently obvious that this would be a long war, both on land and at sea.

Stalemate on land and at sea, along with the prospect of a long conflict in which economic and financial endurance would overshadow prowess on the battlefield as the arbiter of war, set the stage for a major and fateful redefinition of Germany's submarine strategy. Thanks to the invention of the submarine, commerce warfare, so long disdained by naval strategists in and out of uniform as "a delusion, and a most dangerous delusion," displaced the "decisive battle" as the centerpiece of naval strategic thinking. The immediate trigger for the three-month-long debate that followed between Germany's naval and political leadership was a British announcement, on 2 October 1914, that in order to protect cross-Channel traffic against U-boats, the eastern approaches had been barred with a minefield.[56] During the first month after the declaration, 2,764 mines were planted; another 4,390 were laid during the first two weeks of February the following year.[57]

A *Denkschrift* (memorandum) by the commander of the *U-boot* forces, *Korevetten-kapitän* Hermann Bauer, framed Germany's fateful debate. He called for immediate retaliation by using the underwater weapon against British commerce.[58] His superior officers at the High Sea Fleet and on the admiralty staff were sympathetic. The commander of the 2nd Battle Squadron, Admiral Reinholdt Scheer, insisted that if this new and powerful weapon was going to be used to full effect, it must be done "in the way most suited to its peculiarities"—that is, without warning and without sparing the crews of the victimized steamers.[59] But while the navy's uniformed leadership were naturally focused on the potential military effectiveness of a ship-sinking offensive, the country's political leadership worried about the possible political consequences, especially the reaction of the neutral countries, first and foremost the United States. Imperial chancellor Theobald von Bethmann-Hollweg told the navy that there were no legal objections to a commerce campaign but that a decision to go ahead should await a stronger German military position on land. In the event, Germany need not worry how the neutrals might react. Scheer's comment written after the war fairly sums up the navy's frustration: "Enemies on all sides! That was the situation."[60]

The pressure to find an alternative military solution to the stalemate on land continued. In the Reichstag, Bethmann-Hollweg came under strong criticism for hindering the U-boats and being soft on the British.[61] The press too clamored for retaliation against Britain's "illegal" blockade.[62] On 21 November *Grossadmiral* Alfred von Tirpitz, the "father" of the High Sea Fleet, asked an American reporter the rhetorical question whether Germany did not have as much right as the British opponent to "starve us out" and retaliate "by torpedoing any of their ships and their Allies' ships."[63] Bethmann-Hollweg reluctantly conceded on 1 February 1915. The High Sea Fleet's commander in chief, Admiral von Pohl, had assured him that the U-boats would have no difficulty telling enemy from neutral vessels and that just to make sure, very strict rules of engagement (ROE) would be issued.[64] Two days later, the announcement came that, starting 18 February, all the waters around the British Isles and the Channel would be a "war zone," in which all enemy ships would be destroyed and neutrals would "navigate at their peril."[65] American protests quickly compelled the Germans to exempt all neutral vessels, hospital ships, and vessels of the Commission for the Relief of Belgium.[66]

The U-boats' restrictive ROE effectively forestalled the kind of anti-commerce campaign originally envisaged. Strategically, the exemption of neutrals meant that roughly 30 percent of British seagoing trade was immune from attack. Tactically, this translated into a much less target-rich environment for the U-boats. Also, the requirement that the U-boat commander make sure of the national identity of a ship before it could be sunk made his task much more complicated. On the one hand, the captain's instructions told him that his "first consideration is the safety of the submarine."[67] Yet the ROE also told him he could carry out his mission only after he had come to the surface and made a positive identification of the ship's nationality at close range (within enemy gun range).[68] It did not take the British long to exploit this contradiction.

The U-boat order of battle at the beginning of what became known as the "first offensive" stood at about thirty, a small net increase since the start of the war.[69] Even this small number practically overstates the size of the force that was given the task of bringing Britain to the bargaining table. To begin with, not all boats were available for operations at any given time; some were used for training, while others would be undergoing refit and repair. Next, up to twelve boats were initially withheld for the defense of the High Sea Fleet's home waters.[70] This meant that once the offensive got under way, no more than twenty-four boats were available. According to Scheer, this translated into three or four standing patrols astride Britain's main trade routes.[71]

It is not surprising that, given this small number and ROE that effectively forced the U-boats to fight a "prize war" according to prerevolutionary Mahanian rules of war *on the sea*, the return in merchant shipping sunk in the first offensive was not impressive: 154 British vessels were lost to U-boats between February and the end of September.[72] Fortunately for the Germans, U-boat losses were small as well; nineteen were lost during the same period, but only thirteen of those have definitely been attributed to hostile action of one sort or another.[73] This result is somewhat surprising when it is realized that 120 of the 154 ships that fell victim were "captured"—that is, sunk according to the prize rules. This means that almost 80 percent of the (successful) attacks occurred with the U-boat stationary and fully exposed on the surface. Corbett's authorized history of the war at sea took note how the relatively low shipping losses during this first U-boat offensive led many to believe that the "defence had mastered the attack."[74] The truth is that the failure of the first offensive had far less to do with the efficiency of British defensive measures than the U-boats' self-imposed restrictions.

Notes

1. The chapter title is from *Boston Journal*, 2 June 1901, cited in Alan H. Burgoygne, *Submarine Navigation Past and Present* (New York: E. P. Dutton, 1903), vol. 2, p. 350.

2. Cited in U.S. Naval Institute *Proceedings* [hereafter *USNIP*] (March 1899), p. 247.

3. Gérard Garier, *L'odyssée technique et humaine du sous-marin en France, Tome 1: Du Plongeur (1863) aux Guêpe (1904)* (Bourg en Bresse, Fr.: Marines edition, 1995).

4. *USNIP* (June 1900), p. 380.

5. Cited in "Successful Trials of the Holland Submarine Boat," *USNIP* (December 1899), p. 925.

6. Cited in Nicholas Lambert, *The Submarine Service, 1900–1918* (Aldershot: Ashgate for the Navy Records Society, 2001), p. 11.

7. Senior Naval Lord, minute, 4 May 1900, cited in ibid., p. 8.

8. William Laird Clowes, the author of a seven-volume history of the Royal Navy, commented at the time that, experimentation being the purpose, there was little point in going ahead with the purchase. Why risk officers and crew, he asked, when technology was about to allow the creation of remotely controlled, unmanned vessels and weapons, called "actinauts"? William Laird Clowes, *The Royal Navy: A History from the Earliest Times to 1900* (London: Sampson Low, Marston, 1903; repr. Chatham, 1997), vol. 7, p. 62.

9. Willem Hackmann, *Seek & Strike: Sonar, Anti-submarine Warfare and the Royal Navy 1914–54* (London: H.M. Stationery Off., 1984), pp. 7–10.

10. Admiral Bacon reports in his post–World War I account of his command of the "Dover Patrol" how, before the war, mines were "viewed askance . . . since we, the strongest Power, always fostered the idea that it was

our business to tempt the enemy to come out and fight, and not block him in." Admiral Sir Reginald Bacon, *The Dover Patrol 1915–1917* (London: Hutchinson, 1919), vol. 1, p. 109.

11. Capt. J. S. Cowie, *Mines, Minelayers and Minelaying* (London: Oxford Univ. Press, 1949), p. 31.

12. Dwight R. Messimer, *Find and Destroy: Antisubmarine Warfare in World War I* (Annapolis, Md.: Naval Institute Press, 2001), pp. 51–55.

13. Ibid., pp. 55–56.

14. Admiral of the Fleet Lord Fisher, memorandum, 5th edition printed May 1914, cited in Lambert, *Submarine Service 1900–1918,* p. 215.

15. National Archives, Kew, U.K., ADM 116/ 1043B, P. II, "Distribution of British Naval Forces in Outlaying Stations in Relation to the Protection of British Maritime Commerce in War with Germany," handwritten note, "Anticipated German Operations of War." The ADM files at the British National Archives (formerly known as Public Record Office) refer to Admiralty records.

16. Admiral Sir Percy Scott, *Fifty Years in the Royal Navy* (London: John Murray, 1919), pp. 287–88.

17. According to the Declaration of London of 1909, enemy civilian shipping could be destroyed only after crew and passengers had been placed in safety—which meant, in practical terms, placed on board the warship. Neutral ships, if caught with contraband on board, could not be destroyed but could be taken as prizes. See Messimer, *Find and Destroy,* p. 4.

18. Cited in Lambert, *Submarine Service 1900–1918,* p. 232. Interestingly, Fisher himself thought that, between its geographic disadvantages and its much smaller merchant fleet, Germany was much more vulnerable to Britain's submarine fleet than vice versa.

19. Captain Herbert S. Richmond—later Admiral Richmond and prominent naval commentator—reportedly cited the submarine's technical difficulties in abiding by the prize laws as evidence that it made a poor commerce raider. Reported in Arthur J. Marder, *From the Dreadnought to Scapa Flow* (London: Oxford Univ. Press, 1961), vol. 1, p. 364, cited in Angus Ross, "Losing the Initiative in Mercantile Warfare: Great Britain's Surprising Failure to Anticipate Maritime Challenges to Her Global Trading Network in the First World War," *International Journal of Naval History* 1, no. 1 (April 2002), available at www.ijnhonline.org.

20. Admiralty note, 30 April 1905, cited in Ruddock F. Mackay, *Fisher of Kilverstone* (Oxford, U.K.: Clarendon, 1973), p. 340.

21. Cited in Archibald Hurd, *The Merchant Navy* (London: John Murray, 1921), vol. 1, p. 214.

22. National Archives, Kew, U.K., ADM 116/ 1043B, Pt. 1, "War Plan—Germany. W.1. Ch. II, 'Anticipated German Operations of War.'"

23. Ibid.

24. National Archives, Kew, U.K., ADM 137/ 2831, *Trade Division Records: Losses of Merchant Ships,* "Memorandum on Possible Losses to British Commerce in an Anglo-German War," 28 May 1914.

25. Col. à Court Repington, "New Wars for Old: I. The Submarine Menace," *Blackwood's Magazine* (June 1910), cited in http:// www.archive.org/texts/flipbook/flippy.php?id =blackwoodsmagazi187edinuoft.

26. Ibid.

27. Lambert, *Submarine Service 1900–1918,* pp. 125–26.

28. Admiral Scheer, *Germany's High Sea Fleet in the World War* (London: Cassell, 1920), p. xiii.

29. For example, in an article in the August 1908 issue of the *Deutsche Revue,* retired vice admiral Freiherr von Schleinitz urged the building of a fleet of large U-boats capable of sinking English merchant ships. Doing so, he wrote, would be "much more significant than defeating the opponent in a naval battle." Von Schleinitz, "Der Außen- und Kleinkrieg zur See und seine Bedeutung für Deutschland," *Deutsche Revue* 33, no. 3 (1908), pp. 132–49, cited in Joachim Schröder, *Die U-Boote des Kaisers* (Bonn: Bernard and Graefe Verlag, 2003), pp. 27–28.

30. A few months before the outbreak of war, a certain *Korvettenkapitän* (Lieutenant) Ulrich-Eberhard Blum of the navy's Submarine Inspectorate at Kiel published a memorandum estimating that a minimum of 222 submarines were needed to undertake an effective blockade against Britain. Blum's calculation proved surprisingly prescient,

but his commanding officer ruled that the matter was not yet ripe for discussion. Arno Spindler, *Der Krieg zur See 1914–1918: Der Handelskrieg mit U-booten*, vol. 1, *Vorgeschichte* (Berlin: E. S. Mittler and Son, 1932) cited in Carl-Axel Gemzell, *Organization, Conflict, and Innovation: A Study of German Naval Strategic Planning, 1888–1940* (Stockholm: Esselte Studium, 1973), p. 62.

31. None of the "standard" sources on German pre–World War I military or naval planning report the existence of operational or contingency plans for a large-scale U-boat commerce war. See Gemzell, *Organization, Conflict, and Innovation;* Paul M. Kennedy, "The Development of German Naval Operations Plans against England, 1896–1914," *The War Plans of the Great Powers 1880–1914*, ed. Kennedy (London: Unwin Hyman, 1979), pp. 171–98; and Ivo Nikolai Lambdi, *The Navy and German Power Politics, 1862–1914* (Boston: Allen and Unwin, 1984).

32. Theodore Ropp, *The Development of a Modern Navy: French Naval Policy, 1871–1904* (Annapolis, Md.: Naval Institute Press, 1987), pp. 155–80.

33. Gabriel Charmes, *La réforme de la marine* (Paris: Ancienne Maison Michel Lévy Frères, 1868), pp. 124–25, cited in Capitaine de frégate Raoul Castex, *Synthèse de la Guerre Sous-Marine de Pontchartrain à Tirpiz* (Paris: Librairie Maritime et Coloniale, 1920), p. 26.

34. Admiral Aube in *L'Atlas Coloniale* (1889), cited in Castex.

35. Ropp, *Development of a Modern Navy,* p. 170.

36. The improvement in torpedo speed became possible when the switch was made, around 1905, to superheated compressed air instead of cold air for propulsion. See Geoff Kirby, "A History of the Torpedo in the Early Days," *Journal of the Royal Navy Scientific Service,* vol. 27:1, pp. 19–20. The article can be found on http://www.btinernet.com/~philipr/torps .htm.

37. See Louis C. Gerken, *Torpedo Technology* (Chula Vista, Calif.: American Scientific Corp., 1989), esp. pp. 1–36; and Eberhard Rössler, *The U-boat: The Evolution and Technical History of German Submarines* (Annapolis, Md.: Naval Institute Press, 1981), p. 344.

38. E. M. Cumming, "A Short History of Torpedoes 1866–1944," *Weymouth Diving Web,* www.weymouthdiving.co.uk/torphist.htm, p. 12.

39. *Krab* was not completed until 1915. See Jan S. Breemer, *Soviet Submarines: Design, Development, and Tactics* (Coulsdon, U.K.: Jane's Information Group, 1989), pp. 22–23.

40. See Arthur Hezlet, *Electronics and Sea Power* (New York: Stein and Day, 1975), pp. 97, 298. Also, Lt. C. W. Nimitz, "Military Value and Tactics of Modern Submarines," *USNIP* (December 1912), p. 1194.

41. *Korvettenkapitän* Albert Bauer, *Die Deutschen U-boote in ihrer Kriegsführung 1914–1918*, vol. 2, *Die U-Bootsblockade Februar bis Oktober 1915* (Berlin: E. S. Mittler and Son, 1920), pp. 14–15, 41. The author had commanded the High Sea Fleet's 3rd U-boat Flotilla.

42. Patrick Beesly, *Room 40: British Naval Intelligence 1914–1918* (New York: Harcourt Brace Jovanovich, 1982), p. 30.

43. Ibid., p. 91. Also, Robert M. Grant, *U-boat Intelligence 1914–1918* (Hamden, Conn.: Archon Books, 1969), pp. 17–18.

44. Beesly, *Room 40,* p. 254.

45. National Archives, Kew, U.K., ADM116/ 1430, *Report on the Present Organisation of the Board of Invention and Research* [better known as the Holland Report, after its main contributor, Sir R. Sothern Holland].

46. The subheading is from *Punch* (London), July 1917. Reprinted in *Mr. Punch's History of the Great War* (London: Cassell and Co., 1919), p. 163.

47. Robert M. Grant, *U-boats Destroyed: The Effect of Anti-submarine Warfare 1914–1918* (London: Putnam, 1964), pp. 17–18.

48. Rössler, *U-boat,* p. 36.

49. Sir Julian S. Corbett, *Naval Operations* (London: Longmans, Green, 1921), vol. 1, p. 182.

50. National Archives, Kew, U.K., ADM 116/ 1341, *Grand Fleet Battle Orders August 1914– May 31st 1916*, "Grand Fleet Battle Orders amendment of 23/2/15."

51. National Archives, Kew, U.K., ADM 116/ 1341, *Grand Fleet Battle Orders August 1914– May 31st 1916*, "Grand Fleet Battle Orders in Force at Battle of Jutland May 31st 1916."

52. Ibid., p. 80.

53. *Koervettenkapitän* D. Groos, *Der Krieg in der Nordsee*, vol. 3, *Von Ende November 1914 bis*

Anfang Februar 1915 (Berlin: E. S. Mittler and Son, 1922), app. 3, "Gedanken über die zukünftige Führung des Seekrieges" [Thoughts on the Future Conduct of the Naval War], p. 263.

54. Ibid.

55. The dominant expectation among professional military men and the public alike that this would be a short war is reflected in, for example, the British plan of 1912 for the wartime use of the country's shipbuilding resources. It was predicated on a six-month conflict. See P. Haggie, "The Royal Navy and War Planning in the Fisher Era," in *War Plans of the Great Powers 1880–1914,* ed. Kennedy, p. 130. Admiral of the Fleet Lord Chatfield later recalled how nearly everyone believed the war would not last long, for "the financiers told us, and they must know; they had lectured us as had the economists in our war courses." Admiral of the Fleet Lord Chatfield, *The Navy and Defence* (London: William Heinemann, 1942), p. 120.

56. Sir Julian S. Corbett, *Naval Operations,* vol. 1, p. 182. The prospective arrival of U-boats at the German-occupied Belgian harbors of Zeebrugge and Ostend was, no doubt, a major factor in the British decision. On 9 November 1914 the first U-boat *(U-12)* arrived at Zeebrugge. The "Flanders U-boat Flotilla" was formally stood up on 15 March 1915 and at one point counted thirty-seven submarines. See Johan Ryheul, "The Flandern U-boat Bases and U-Bootflottille Flandern," *Uboat.net 1995–2010.* The report can be found on http://www.uboat.net.

57. Günter Krause, *U-Boot Alarm: Zur Geschichte der U-Boot-Abwehr (1914–1945)* (Berlin: Brandenburgische Verlagshaus, 1998), p. 34.

58. Gemzell, *Organization, Conflict, and Innovation,* p. 142.

59. Scheer, *Germany's High Sea Fleet in the World War,* p. 222.

60. Ibid., p. 223.

61. Messimer, *Find and Destroy,* p. 16.

62. For the German media's demand for submarine commerce raiding, see Gemzell, *Organization, Conflict, and Innovation,* p. 143.

63. Sir Julian S. Corbett, *Naval Operations* (London: Longmans, Green, 1921), vol. 2, p. 132.

64. Messimer, *Find and Destroy,* p. 17.

65. Ibid.

66. Grant, *U-boats Destroyed,* p. 21.

67. John Terrain, *The U-boat Wars 1916–1945* (New York: Henry Holt, 1989), p. 9.

68. The controversy over how much risk should be accepted in order to ensure discriminative targeting continues—witness the contemporary debate over the trade-off between (expensive) precision bombing and the minimization of collateral damage.

69. Grant, *U-boats Destroyed* (p. 20), calculates an order of battle of thirty; Paul G. Halpern, *A Naval History of World War I* (Annapolis, Md.: Naval Institute Press, 1995), p. 294, reports a total thirty-seven, with twenty-five available for blockade duties; Scheer wrote in *Germany's High Sea Fleet* (p. 257) that about twenty-four were available; and Rössler's *U-boat* (p. 47) asserts that twenty-seven boats were available on 1 April.

70. Arno Spindler, *Der Krieg zur See 1914–1918: Der Handelskrieg mit U-Booten,* vol. 2, *Februar bis September 1915* (Berlin: E. S. Mittler and Son, 1933; trans. Naval War College as *The War at Sea, 1914–1918: The Submarine War on Commerce* [Newport, R.I.: Department of Intelligence and Research, 1934]), chap. 1, p. 3.

71. Scheer, *Germany's High Sea Fleet in the World War,* p. 257.

72. *Merchant Shipping (Losses)* (London: H.M. Stationery Off., 1919), reprinted in *British Vessels Lost at Sea 1914–18, Section II: Merchant Shipping (Losses)* (Cambridge, U.K.: Patrick Stevens, 1977), pp. 4–11. The number is somewhat higher if losses due to mines laid by U-boats are included.

73. Grant, *U-boats Destroyed,* pp. 11–16.

74. Sir Julian S. Corbett, *Naval Operations* (London: Longmans, Green, 1923), vol. 3, p. 140.

CHAPTER TWO

Cutting the Thin Thread

When he wrote the official British history of the war at sea, Corbett noted that Tirpitz's November 1914 interview seemed an empty threat at the time, one that required "no special measures."[1] In reality, as it became increasingly evident that the war would last at least another year and that the U-boats' activities would amount to more than a nuisance, "special measures" were in fact taken. They were of two kinds. The first were immediate measures using existing technologies and capabilities to, if not destroy the submerged enemy, at least limit his freedom of maneuver and effectiveness. These steps would, it was hoped, keep the U-boats' depredations to a tolerable level, while science and technology tried to find a long-term solution by way of new kinds of weapons and, more important, means of detection. Underlying this overall strategy was the assumption that the only way to defeat the U-boat menace was by *sinking* it.

Immediate measures taken on the eve of the U-boats' first offensive started with the division of Britain's home waters into twenty-three patrol zones, each guarded by a collection of "low-tech" patrol vessels—trawlers, drifters, private yachts.[2] The Dover Patrol quickly became one of the war's most important organizations of the kind. This motley fleet—which later became the "Auxiliary Patrol"—was at first charged only with reporting a suspected submarine to the nearest "Naval Centre." This site would then contact the closest naval forces for the actual pursuit and engagement. The problem was that should a patrol be lucky enough to spot a U-boat, it probably would not have a radio. Even if it did, the chances were small that enough destroyers would be near enough to respond in time to pick up the hunt. Consequently, the patrols themselves were eventually turned into hunters, first with guns and later depth charges. In terms of numbers, the scale of the effort was massive; in January 1915 more than eight hundred auxiliary patrol vessels plied Britain's coastal waters. As far as is known, however, only three U-boats fell victim to their activities during the entire war.[3]

Drifters and yachts were also enlisted in the establishment of an elaborate barrier of mines and "Bircham indicator nets" across the Strait of Dover. The idea here was to prevent the U-boats from infesting the "focal points" of shipping between London and the Irish Sea. During the first two weeks of February more than 4,300 mines were planted between Dunkirk and the Thames estuary.[4] Next, the fields were complemented by some sixteen miles of indicator nets. Made of wide-mesh steel wire, the nets had two purposes: first, they would, it was hoped, act as a trip wire for the vessels patrolling above. The idea was that a penetrating submarine would tear off a portion of the net, entangle itself, and betray its position by dragging the attached buoys. The alerted patrol vessel was then supposed to ram or bomb the hapless U-boat. Alternatively, a "smart" U-boat commander who tried to avoid the nets would do so by diving into the mines below.

The "Dover Barrage," as it came to be known, had mixed results. To begin with, it was soon realized that the indicator nets could not stand up to the Channel's strong currents and stormy weather (as Admiral Bacon put it, "It is one thing to theorise and devise obstructions at a drawing board, calculating the statical stresses, and another to see that structure in a seaway with a strong tide running").[5] Nets were repeatedly cut loose, requiring constant maintenance and repair. Plans were then made to add stronger sub-marine nets, but most of the materials were diverted to operations in the Dardanelles in March 1915; the work really did not get under way until September.[6] The mines had their own share of problems. It was not long before both sides were aware that British sea mines often looked more intimidating than they were in fact. The moorings were weak, so that the devices had a habit of breaking loose in even moderately adverse weather (and endangering friendly shipping as a result), and the firing devices were notoriously unreliable.[7] Not until 1917—thanks to the technical assistance of Britain's Russian ally—was the production of an effective family of mines taken in hand.[8]

The barrier's technical shortfalls were aggravated by the British failure to support its static portion with adequate patrol forces. As long as the Grand Fleet had first call on the most capable destroyers, patrols that were supposed to watch for intruders remained short on both quality and quantity.[9] To make matters worse, until late 1917 the patrols kept their watches only in daylight hours and during the good season—that is, May to November. The indicator nets too had to be pulled in at night.[10] As a result, the Dover Barrage could claim only a single U-boat before November 1917, when better mines, some based on captured German designs, became available and around-the-clock patrols were established.

The British were aware of the barrage's problems by the spring of 1915. It did not take the Germans much longer, but for a while, after one U-boat had gotten caught in the netting, the barrage served as a fairly effective deterrent. Namely, the Heligoland-based U-boats were instructed to sail for patrol stations in the Irish Sea by way of the much

longer trip around northern Scotland. It can therefore be said that though the barrage
was not particularly proficient as a system for destroying submarines, it did contribute
to the ASW effort by restricting the U-boat's *productivity.*[11]

As the British struggled to come to grips with the new weapon of war by conventional
methods, they were increasingly compelled to resort to *un*conventional tactics. Some of
these tactics arguably violated prevailing customs and rules of war at sea. The arming
of merchantmen for specifically offensive anti-U-boat operations is a case in point.
Consistent with British plans before the war, selected civilian ships were armed with
guns immediately at the start of hostilities; the expectation then still was that so-called
first-class liners would be attractive targets for armed surface raiders. The program
picked up speed when it became evident that the U-boats had shifted focus from "legitimate" warships to merchant vessels. By the end of 1915, 766 merchantmen had been
armed with guns.[12] Although the British government had assured neutrals that the
weapons were for self-defense only and would not be fired unless the vessels carrying
them were fired upon, confidential instructions called for a merchantman to open fire
if its master decided that a spotted U-boat had hostile intentions, even if it had not
fired a weapon.[13] Gun crews were uniformed Royal Navy personnel.[14] In practice, the
use of armed merchant steamers as U-boat killers was a failure; not a single boat was
sunk in this manner. From a different and broader point of view, however, the tactic
had some value: U-boats were more likely to break off an encounter and leave the scene
when they encountered resistance. As a consequence, an armed merchantman was less
likely to be attacked and sunk than an unarmed vessel.[15]

Decoy, or "mystery," ships were another step in the "militarization" of civilian shipping.
Also known as "Q-ships," these were freighters and colliers manned by Royal Navy crews
and fitted with concealed guns but deliberately camouflaged to look harmless. Some
sailed under neutral flags. Under a program begun in November 1914, the purpose was
to lure an unsuspecting U-boat—still fighting according to the Prize Regulations—into
approaching close enough to send a boarding party to row across and inspect the manifest and then, while the submarine was at its most vulnerable, suddenly open fire. The
nearly two hundred British decoy vessels that saw service during the war were responsible for the destruction of altogether thirteen U-boats.[16] They paid a high price however;
thirty-eight Q-ships were lost to various forms of hostile action.[17]

A more sophisticated ruse involved the combination of an "innocent" trawler and submarine. The idea was that the trawler, with a submerged British submarine in tow,
would be approached by a U-boat. The trawler would signal the underwater escort via
a telephone line that ran along the towline, then cast off the tow so the submarine

could position itself for a torpedo attack on the U-boat. There are two known success-ful cases of this early form of submarine-against-submarine combat.[18]

"A Struggle of Inventions"

At least as important as the submarine's revolutionary impact on the nature and con-duct of war at sea was its contribution to the gradual blurring of the traditional divid-ing line between combatants and noncombatants.[19] "Total war" has been one of the distinguishing characteristics of warfare since the beginning of the twentieth century. The Germans took the first step with the declaration that British merchant vessels were now to be sunk without warning; the British responded, further obscuring the distinc-tion between "targetable" military combatants and "nontargetable" civilians, by effec-tively encouraging armed merchant vessels to defend themselves "actively." By the end of the war, after both sides had turned to bombing the opponent's towns and cities rou-tinely from the sea or from the air, few of the old, preindustrial-warfare inhibitions against the killing of civilians and destruction of their property were left. In the next world war, the immunity of noncombatants from deliberate military violence would not even be an issue.

Equally portentous for the future was the role the U-boat now played in changing the relationship between science and war. As the first phase in the U-boats' campaign to cut Britain's sea lines of communications unfolded, even the most optimistic of the Royal Navy's planners had to admit that nets, ramming, and mines, originally meant to sink surface ships, were simply not good enough for dealing with a submarine threat that was becoming more potent by the day. They constituted a makeshift defense whose success depended largely on chance and surprise. It had been thrown together to con-tain the danger long enough for the issue to be settled quickly elsewhere, either by the armies on land or at sea between two battle fleets. When it became evident that Ger-many's shipyards had embarked on a massive submarine-building program, there could be little doubt that the U-boats would be much more than a tactical nuisance that, albeit after some difficulties, could be dealt with in stride by the navy's professionals.[20] At hand instead was a *strategic* problem that defied the tried-and-proven methods of war on the sea. If the submarine represented a novel form of warfare, a systematic defensive effort for the long haul called for equally novel countermeasures whose nature lay as yet outside the experience of the professional naval officer. It might be true that science could do little to help win a "short" war, but without a scientific com-mitment to solving the submarine problem, the end of the war might well come too soon, at least from the British point of view. Hints that Germany's military prowess was indebted in good part to what was believed to be strong collaboration between its military and its centers of scientific research spurred the British into action.

In July 1915, the Advisory Council for Scientific and Industrial Research was established, with the goal of closer integration between the country's war-connected industries and scientific talent. A similar arrangement with a focus on the navy's technological needs was set up within the Admiralty. Named the Board of Invention and Research (BIR), it was made responsible for "assuring for the Admiralty, during the continuance of the war, expert assistance in organizing and encouraging scientific effort in relation to the requirements of the Naval Services."[21] Its first chairman was Admiral "Jackie" Fisher, who a few months earlier had resigned as First Sea Lord.[22] Fisher, of course, had been one of the few voices before the war warning of the submarine as the up-and-coming weapon of sea warfare. Other members eventually included some four dozen scientists in different fields, most notably the Nobel Prize–winning physicist Sir Ernest Rutherford. They were organized into six science and technology sections, of which Section II, Submarines and Wireless Telegraphy, quickly assumed the greatest prominence.[23] During its two-year existence, 14,655, or more than a third, of the 41,127 "inventions" submitted to the board for screening dealt with submarines, antisubmarine defenses, or wireless telegraphy.[24]

That said, it is difficult to tell how much the BIR's work actually contributed to a scientific solution of the submarine problem. One difficulty is that the board's work was mainly preoccupied with evaluating the ideas and inventions of others and funding those it found deserving. Evidently the BIR rarely initiated its own research projects. Section II's most productive work was reportedly done on acoustic research. This field received by far the lion's share of the BIR's expenditures on research grants, £17,048.[25] This does not strike us today like a particularly generous amount, especially when it is realized that a battleship cost about three million pounds to build, or 175 times as much. It could be, of course, that, given this was scientific terra incognita, more luxurious funding could not have been spent productively. In any case, many of the findings of the BIR's acoustic research would be the basis of postwar work, but it had little practical significance for the primitive hydrophone systems built during the First World War. A more immediate contribution to the anti-U-boat effort came from the work of Section II scientists attached to the navy's hydrophone experimental station at Hawkcraig, in northern Scotland. Here the navy's first-generation portable hydrophones were developed.[26]

The BIR was abolished in September 1917 and its work moved to a newly established Central Research Establishment, which was overseen by a newly created Admiralty Department of Experiments and Research (DER). The change came in the wake of the cabinet-commissioned "Holland Report" on the navy's ASW research efforts.[27] In a scathing criticism of the service's lack of prewar preparedness to deal with the submarine, the report noted that "science is only now called in to explore these fields [of acoustic detection]," but that "even at this late stage of the war it is not considered that the problem is now being grappled with sufficient earnestness or with sufficient vigour."[28]

At the root of the report's criticism of what its authors saw as the disappointing progress of the navy's scientific battle against the submarine were the "birthing pangs" that accompanied the birth of the revolutionary new partnership between the world of the military and that of the civilian scientists. The two shared the same objective, but their problem-solving approaches were very different. As the historian of the British navy's early sonar research has explained, there was a fundamental clash of attitudes, which pitted the navy's insistence on pragmatic, trial-and-error research and development against the BIR's insistence on fundamental research. The service's philosophy was one of "satisficing"—finding and going ahead with solutions that, if not perfect, were good enough. The scientists, by contrast, tended to look for the best possible results—theirs was a "value-maximizing" philosophy. Both approaches had their strengths and weaknesses. The navy's more practical approach could sometimes produce results very rapidly; with a war on, waiting for the perfect solution—which might not even exist—could spell disaster. More often, though, this pragmatism resulted in costly failures and waste of resources that, from the scientists' perspective, could have been put to better use in a search for solutions grounded in scientifically "sound" research.

One consequence of this disagreement on how the insights of science should be applied to the immediate operational problems of war was a mutual lack of sympathy for the other side's needs and contributions. The scientists did not always understand the real world of fleet operations, which bore little resemblance to the carefully controlled environment of the laboratory or test range. Conversely, the navy was not always very forthcoming with the kinds of operational data the scientists needed or eager to divert its war-fighting assets, such as ships, for "impractical" experimental purposes.

In Britain and elsewhere after the war, drastic cuts in military expenditures were to bring a substantial scaling-back of the still-embryonic partnership between the military and science. Twenty years later, many of the lessons that had been learned would have to be relearned to fight another world war. Nevertheless, the most important lesson was taken to heart: the balance of military power in future wars, be it at sea, on land, or, now, in the air, would depend as much on the innovativeness of an organized program of science and research as it did on numbers or divisions or fleets of ships. The struggle to defuse the revolutionary impact of the submarine on the old and familiar "rules" of war at sea during World War I served to change forever the historically "standoffish" relationship between science and the military. Before World War I, important technological innovations had almost always been introduced into the military—frequently reluctantly—because of the *push* of inventors in the civilian world. Thus, none of the

big new naval technologies of the late nineteenth and early twentieth centuries—
whether the torpedo, wireless, the aircraft, or the submarine itself—made its appearance in response to a defined military "need." Now, the inability of the familiar,
prerevolutionary means of sea fighting to cope with the submarine and, perhaps more
important, the incapacity of navies to find solutions inside their own institutions compelled them to turn to the research and development "community" and *pull* for
solutions.[29]

On 18 September 1915, the German navy's new chief of staff, Vice Admiral Henning
von Holtzendorff, ordered the cessation of all anti-merchant operations in the English
Channel and off Britain's west coast. The tonnage-sinking campaign would continue in
the North and Mediterranean seas, but only according to the Prize Regulations. The
decision came in the wake of an acrimonious debate among Germany's naval and military leadership, on the one hand, and the emperor and his foreign policy advisers, on
the other. At issue was how to continue fighting the commerce war against Britain in
the face of mounting U.S. pressure over its conduct. The emperor had "suggested" that
a shift in operational focus from Britain's western approaches to the Mediterranean
would minimize the chance of further diplomatic complications with the United States.
The naval leadership was left with little choice; vacating the principal "funnels" of Britain's overseas shipping was the only sensible option, given the increasingly restrictive
ROE of the past few months. On 6 June, following the sinking of *Lusitania,* U-boat
commanders were prohibited from attacking any large passenger ship, neutral or
enemy.[30] A couple of months later the order was expanded to include all passenger liners, regardless of size. Meanwhile, U-boat commanders had been put on notice that in
order to avoid political complications with neutrals, they could only attack a ship when
it had been identified irrefutably as enemy.[31] "In doubtful cases," the order wrote, "it
would be better to let an enemy merchantman pass through than to sink a neutral."[32]

When he announced the "halt" order to his staff, von Holtzendorff confessed that with
this mode of U-boat warfare "we don't even scratch the skin of the whale."[33] On the
face of it, the results so far seemed to hold out little prospect of a quick British collapse.
From January through September 1915, a total five hundred nonmilitary vessels, with
an aggregate tonnage of just over 800,000, had been sunk by the U-boats; about one-
sixth had been sunk without warning.[34] The two numbers put together suggest that a
large percentage of sinkings involved small coastal vessels and fishing boats, whose
losses had relatively little impact on Britain's trade position. The ships that mattered
were the oceangoing vessels of at least 1,600 tons.[35] The historian Dwight Messimer
suggests that about half of the U-boats' sinkings during 1915 as a whole involved the
latter.[36] Compared with Britain's overall shipping inventory in 1915 of some twenty-
one million tons, even the entire 800,000-ton figure was far from life threatening. It

must also be remembered that many of the British losses up to this point could be off-set by enemy and neutral ships taken as prizes.[37] In fact, according to one author, the British booty of 743 merchantmen in 1914 and 1915 exceeded the number of ships sunk so far in those years by the U-boats.[38]

The U-boats paid a heavy prize in return. Altogether nineteen boats fell victim to enemy action in 1915; sixteen were lost in the waters around the British Isles.[39] It could be said that when the five boats lost in 1914 are added, Germany had effectively lost the entire underwater fleet it had possessed at the start of the war. Of course, the construc-tion of new submarines had not stood still. Fifty-two new boats were placed into ser-vice during 1915; by the end of the year forty-four boats were available for frontline duty.[40] On the British side, even though the year's losses were tolerable—average monthly losses in ships and tonnage had so far been kept to 1 percent or less—indica-tions were that the numbers would likely rise and eventually have a serious impact on the nation's economic life in general and the war effort in particular. As the author of *History of the Great War: Seaborne Trade* puts it, the "situation contained elements of danger which only required time to become more clearly manifest."[41] For one, it was now patently evident that the war would be a very prolonged affair, and it was far from clear which side could outlast the other in a drawn-out economic struggle.[42]

More bad portents were certain trends in ship losses. One was that among the ships that mattered—the oceangoing vessels of at least 1,600 tons—losses had averaged 5 percent.[43] Next, monthly losses in the last two months of the U-boats' first offensive had seen a very sharp increase. Whereas the average monthly British loss during the first seven months of 1915 had been 54,633 tons, August and September recorded losses of 148,464 and 101,690 tons, respectively.[44] What made these figures especially problematic for the future was that they coincided with an alarming drop in new con-struction. According to one authority, 416,000 tons of new merchant shipping were still launched during the last quarter of 1914. The June and September quarters, however, produced only 148,000 and 149,000 tons, respectively—that is, less than had been sunk.[45] Making this picture even worse was the escalating demand for shipping to sup-port the war effort—this could only come at the expense of the national economy. At the start of 1915, about 20 percent of British oceangoing tonnage had been requisi-tioned to support the British and allied military effort.[46] By the end of October, the per-centage had grown to 25, which included 1,450 ships with an aggregate tonnage of more than 5.5 million.[47] Two months later, the allies called for another 1,428,000 tons, which could only be had by reducing Britain's own import needs.[48] In sum, Churchill and others were only partially right when they sought to interpret the U-boats' retreat from the narrow seas as their "first defeat."[49] Defeated the U-boats were indeed, but it

was mainly a self-inflicted defeat that owed little to the tactical or technical efficacy of the defender.

One more set of statistics deserves mention. They were cited by Churchill in his post-war reminiscences to back his claim that the U-boat campaign of 1915 had been defeated. In April of that year, Churchill wrote, the U-boats sank twenty-three ships, only half of which were British. When this paltry number was juxtaposed with the fact that during the same month British ports saw over six thousand arrivals and departures, it was "patent to the whole world" that the Germans had failed miserably.[50] There was only one problem with Churchill's numbers, which would haunt British attempts to come to grips with the submarine until it was almost too late. They made for good propaganda—uplifting morale at home and (it was hoped) deceiving the enemy about his true accomplishments. The problem with Churchill's statistics was that they compared apples and oranges. The six thousand or so arrivals and departures—most were under 1,600 tons—included many vessels that made multiple port calls on a single voyage. This meant that numerous ships were double or even triple counted.

The monthly bulletins did not fool the Germans, who had their own, quite accurate sources of information, but they misled British planners. Initially, mixing numbers of port calls with numbers of individual vessels created a false sense of security about the condition of the country's shipping resources and, as a corollary, helped inflate the estimate of the efficiency of ASW measures. Later, the excessive estimate of the number of oceangoing vessels calling on British ports contributed to the belief that convoying was impractical, that not enough escorts could be provided. It was only in 1917, when Britain reeled under the onslaught of unrestricted submarine warfare, that a couple of relatively junior naval officers pursued the "real" numbers and realized the scale of the self-deception.

The restricted U-boat war against shipping in British waters resumed in February 1916. The commanders' ROE during what became the short-lived "second offensive" differed little from those of the year before: enemy merchant vessels caught inside the war zone could be sunk without warning, neutrals according to the prize rules. Armed enemy merchant vessels were to be treated as auxiliary cruisers and sunk without warning regardless of their whereabouts in or outside the war zone. An exception was made for passenger liners; armed or not, they were off limits.[51] The rules were symptomatic of the compromise that was reached between the naval leadership's insistence on unrestricted warfare and the political leadership's continuing worry over the attitude of Britain's most potent ASW weapon so far—the United States.

The overarching aim of the German campaign this time was to choke off Britain's economic lifeline and force it to the peace table. Two considerations played a role, of which the first was retaliation for Britain's illegal "Hungerblockade." The announcement by Britain's foreign secretary, Sir Edward Grey, in January 1916 of what effectively amounted to a total economic blockade of Germany set off a storm of public and military demands to "unshackle" the U-boats.[52] Next, the current fleet buildup, which added an average of six new boats each month, had opened a window of opportunity to make a possibly decisive impact on British trade.[53] The naval staff claimed that if the U-boats could sink a monthly average of about 630,000 tons of shipping, they could bring Britain to its knees in six to eight months.[54] Bethmann-Hollweg was not impressed. His calculations showed that Britain needed a monthly import of cereals of only fifteen to sixteen thousand tons—an amount that called for only a handful of ships. Furthermore, he wrote in a memorandum dated 29 February 1916, the navy seemed to have ignored the possibility of increased enemy countermeasures, including, ironically, convoying.[55] His cabinet colleague, finance minister Karl Helfferich, joined in, pointing out that the navy's claim that additional American financial aid would not help Britain presumed that an "iron curtain" of U-boats could isolate the island from the rest of the world. Even the navy itself, he said, counted on a slow and gradual reduction of enemy tonnage.[56] In the end, though, it was the fear of a final break with the United States that forced the navy to settle for less than an all-out campaign.

British Countermeasures

As the author of *U-Boot Alarm* put it, the U-boats' second offensive met with few improvements in either the technical or tactical quality of British ASW measures. On the weapons side, the first depth charges were issued to the fleet and the Auxiliary Patrol in January 1916. They would not prove effective until more than a year later. Initial production runs were so small that the ships lucky enough to get any weapons at all were provided only two. Even if more ordnance had been available, the lack of a reliable means of detection would have kept the "probability of kill" extremely low. As long as "targeting" a U-boat depended mainly on where it had been last seen, any chance of success for a craft carrying only a couple of depth charges required that it be almost literally on top of the enemy when it was sighted—that is, within 140 feet of it.[57] It took the introduction of hydrophones and, more important, larger load-outs for saturation attacks to make the depth charge eventually the single most productive U-boat "killer" in World War I.

On the tactical side of the ASW ledger, British efforts in 1916 can best be characterized as "more of the same." The minefields in the Strait of Dover were strengthened, more nets were added, additional decoy ships entered service, and more and more vessels of various types joined the coastal auxiliary patrols. By the end of the year, nearly three thousand vessels were patrolling U-boat-infested waters.[58] The patrols were concentrated mainly along the so-called approach routes, or focal points of merchant shipping. This was where the broad oceanic lanes became narrow funnels and where it was thought the need to protect shipping was greatest and the presence of submarines most likely. There was nothing wrong with this reasoning, but the fact that the problem was understood did not mean it could be *solved*.

The auxiliary patrols, which had originally been intended to alert naval forces to the presence of U-boats, had by this time increasingly assumed an active "hunt and kill" role. The problem was that without some kind of listening gear and more depth charges, the probability of finding, let alone sinking, the enemy remained largely a matter of accident and luck. Jellicoe blamed a shortage of ships to keep the U-boat down and exhaust its batteries as the reason for the "invariable difficulty" of bringing an encounter to successful conclusion.[59] But this was hardly the crux of the matter, as is evident from one hunt-and-kill operation in September 1917. For seven days, two, perhaps three, U-boats sank more than thirty merchantmen in an area off the south coast of England that was being watched over by forty-nine destroyers, forty-eight torpedo boats, and 168 armed auxiliaries. During this time, the underwater enemy was actively hunted by thirteen destroyers and seven Q-ships, which achieved no results.[60]

ASW productivity during the U-boats' 1916 campaign had actually declined compared with the year before. During the four-month second offensive, hostile action accounted for the loss of only four U-boats in British waters—that is, roughly one boat per month, compared with an average of two during the 1915 campaign. This disappointing record particularly stands out in light of two more facts. First, the ASW forces were operating in an environment that was twice as "target rich" as the year before. A monthly average of almost twelve U-boats operated around the British Isles during 1916, about twice as many as in 1915.[61] Second, the number of ships involved in the ASW battle had risen to nearly three thousand. All things being equal, therefore, the chances of an encounter and, by inference, a kill should have been substantially greater, at least twice as high. One reason why this was not the case is that the arming of merchant vessels had made the U-boats far more cautious in approaching their intended victims. They used torpedoes more frequently; when they did not, the boats tended to stand off beyond gun range and use light signals or warning shots to force a surrender. If a ship answered with gunfire, the U-boat, which was now likely to be armed with a mix of two 88-mm and 105-mm guns, could respond in kind and stand a fair chance of outshooting the merchantman's twelve-pounder or four-inch cannon. Alternatively, it could submerge, which an experienced crew could now accomplish in about a minute.[62] All in all, therefore, with the scheme of ASW methods then in existence, the British could count on destroying eighteen to twenty U-boats a year, or between three and four every four months.[63]

On the U-boats' side of the ledger, productivity fell far short of the naval staff's goal of 630,000 tons per month. Between March and May the boats accounted for 215 British vessels, with an aggregate tonnage of almost 480,000.[64] This number averaged out to about the same monthly loss rate of the year before. Nonetheless, due to other pressures on shipping, losses had become more difficult for Britain to absorb. There was a growing allied (including French, Italian, and Russian) demand for shipping; the supply needs of British forces on the western front had skyrocketed, and the output of shipyards had declined, due in part to the Royal Navy's needs for the repair and construction of its own vessels. The numbers are telling. During the first quarter of 1916, 325 British ships were lost from all causes; the yards produced ninety-three new vessels. Two hundred seventy-one vessels were lost in the second quarter; the yards completed 113.[65] All in all, the overall quandary for British shipping in the spring of 1916 can be summed up as this: how to meet the growing demand for war-related carrying capacity with a merchant fleet that was steadily declining in numbers and tonnage. Since cutting back on the flow of war matériel was not an option, the only apparent solution was a drastic reduction in "nonessential" imports.

The "*Sussex* incident" and subsequent U.S. intervention permitted the British, however briefly, to postpone the unpopular decision to impose import restrictions and their corollary, rationing. On 24 March, the Flanders-based *UB-29* sank the French cross-Channel steamer *Sussex*. About fifty passengers and crew were lost, including an undetermined number of Americans. The U-boat attacked the ship with a torpedo, without warning. The hapless German commander insisted he had mistaken the liner for a minelayer, but the neutral nations, especially the United States, accused Germany of deliberately and recklessly violating the ban on attacking unarmed passenger ships. Ironically, the Germans had never publicized their own prohibition against attacking liners, armed or not. President Wilson had accordingly good reason to believe that the *Sussex* incident was proof of a Germany that fully intended to cast off all restrictions. Confronted with the threat of an American diplomatic rupture, the Germans backed down. On 24 April the boats were ordered to return to Prize Regulations. The next day, the commander of the High Sea Fleet, Admiral Scheer, citing the danger of operating under those restrictions, recalled its boats from British home waters. According to Scheer, it was now "left to me until further notice to employ the U-boats in purely military enterprises."[66]

When U-boat operations ceased, the New York daily *Evening Mail* exulted that henceforth "every ship that sails the seas is now as safe as if the submarine had never been invented. Germany lays down the submarine arm."[67] In reality, only the operations by the *attack* boats were halted, and then only in the waters around Britain. The smaller minelaying boats continued their operations, and attacks in the Mediterranean continued uninterrupted.[68] The substantial results achieved there despite the restrictive Prize Regulations (more than 129,000 tons of shipping were sunk in August 1916 alone) were important in the resumption of the campaign in the fall of the year.

During the "pause," the battle of Jutland (Skagerrak, for the Germans) was fought. Fourteen U-boats participated in what many navalists would later decry as Britain's one best (but lost) chance to defeat the U-boat threat once and for all. According to this argument, if the Grand Fleet's commander had only been true to the "Nelsonian spirit" and pursued his enemy, he would almost certainly have sent the bulk of the High Sea Fleet to the bottom of the sea. In that event the U-boats and their "nests" inside the Heligoland Bight would no longer have been protected by the High Sea Fleet's guns and would have been open to a deadly strike from the sea. As one Jutland critic put it, "Had there been a decisive victory for us at Jutland, there certainly would not have been a submarine campaign of 1917, for the submarine campaign was based on the German fleet."[69]

The argument is speculative at best. A sober assessment reveals it as a highly implausible scenario. To begin with, it is not clear at all what a "decisive" British victory would have entailed. At the end of the "real" Jutland, the Grand Fleet's losses in matériel and personnel were about twice as large as the opponent's.[70] A decisive outcome for the British could therefore have come only if Jellicoe's battle fleet had substantially reversed this exchange ratio. Even then, the British would have suffered their own losses, which would have limited their ability to bring power to bear against the U-boat bases. What shape such an operation might have taken is another question. One possibility would have been a close blockade, another an amphibious assault, while a third option could have been a more aggressive minelaying effort. Each would have been a very risky undertaking, as it would have had to be carried out literally under German guns. The island of Heligoland, which dominates the approach into the bight, was heavily defended. Coastal artillery emplacements and the heavy guns of some of Germany's predreadnought battleships covered the coastline. British-laid and German minefields would have made it a slow and tedious task at best to penetrate within striking range of the High Sea Fleet's anchorages at Schilling, Wilhelmshaven, and Altenbruch. Last but certainly not least, the attacker would have had to contend with the guerilla tactics of torpedo boats and U-boats. With respect to the latter, it is important to keep in mind that it was the U-boats, or rather the *fear* of U-boats, that prompted Jellicoe's decision to break off the pursuit at Jutland. In sum, Jellicoe was almost certainly right when, shortly after assuming the post of First Sea Lord, he dismissed calls for a from-the-sea assault against the U-boats as "playing the German game, with the possible result of our losing the command of the sea and the consequent loss of the war."[71]

Although Jutland's outcome was arguably a tactical victory for the Germans, it was clear to Scheer at least that even the most favorable outcome of a decisive battle would not compel the British to sue for peace.[72] It followed, Scheer wrote, that if "we are not finally to be bled to death, full use must be made of the U-boats as a means of war, so as to grip England's vital nerve."[73] Scheer and the navy's leadership asked for the maximum flexibility. The commander of the Flanders flotilla urged that his boats be used to "seal off" the English Channel and sink all shipping there without warning. When this was rejected on political grounds, he grudgingly agreed to fight "this kind of U-boat war," according to the Prize Regulations. It was better than nothing, and he would look upon it as a preparation *(Vorarbeit)* for unrestricted war.[74]

The third (restricted) U-boat offensive lasted from October 1916 to January 1917. During the last quarter of 1916, monthly sinkings exceeded 300,000 tons, for a total of 963,863 tons and 554 ships. This figure was close to the tonnage sunk during the entire preceding year (1,189,031 tons).[75] Several developments made these favorable returns possible. One hundred eight boats were added to the fleet in 1916—nearly five times as many as the number of boats lost (twenty-three). Next, larger boats, U-boat "cruisers," permitted more distant operations, beyond the reach of the coastal auxiliary patrols. Boats were now found in the Gulf of Biscay, from France's Atlantic coast down to Portugal; in the Arctic Sea; and even, on one occasion, off the east coast of the United States.

The rapidly escalating shipping losses in the winter of 1916–17 brought home to Britain's political-military leadership for the first time the fact that it faced a national crisis that could make or break the war effort. Monthly losses were now double those of 1915; shipping under allied flag was being destroyed at a rate of over sixty thousand tons per month, more than three times as fast as the year before. Neutral shipping in particular was being hit hard. In 1915, the neutrals had lost an average of 17,500 tons each month; during the quarter ending in December 1916, no less than 100,000 tons a month disappeared. The situation had, in the words of one author, become "truly alarming."[76] The country's supply of wheat was down to fourteen weeks.[77] Worse, the Admiralty had effectively come to the conclusion that it had no answer to the problem. On 20 November it circulated a memorandum that essentially called on the *army* to solve the problem: "It can definitely be stated that naval resources are practically exhausted as far as small craft for hunting submarines are concerned. . . . It is therefore suggested . . . that the question be considered whether it is not worth while shaping military strategy as far as can now be done to assist in the reduction of the submarine menace through the destruction of as many of their home bases as is practicable."[78]

The seemingly unending litany of military setbacks—the Dardanelles fiasco, the failed Somme offensive, the disappointing outcome of Jutland, and now the U-boat crisis—all contributed to the fall of the Asquith cabinet in December. One of the first decisions of the new prime minister, David Lloyd George, was to institute an inner "War Cabinet," which would, he hoped, streamline the country's unwieldy political-military decision-making process. Placing himself at the War Cabinet's head, Lloyd George appointed Maurice (later Lord) Hankey as its secretary. At its first meeting on 9 December a shipping controller was appointed to give central direction to what had heretofore been the work of a mostly ad hoc collection of agencies that had sprung up to deal with the emergency of the day.[79] Changes were made at the Admiralty as well. Jellicoe was relieved of command of the Grand Fleet and made First Sea Lord. Jellicoe fully agreed with Lloyd George that defeating the U-boats was the number-one priority. As a first step, he brought in one of his Grand Fleet subordinate commanders, Rear Admiral Alexander Ludovic Duff, to head up a new Anti-Submarine Division. The new organization was to coordinate and stimulate all means of defeating the U-boat danger, but Jellicoe's memoirs make patently clear his very traditional and limited understanding of what exactly "defeating the U-boats" meant. "Our object," he wrote, "was to destroy submarines at a greater rate than the output of the German shipyards. This was the surest way of counteracting their activities. It was mainly for the purpose of attack on the submarines that I formed the Anti-Submarine Division of the Naval Staff."[80]

As has been related in the Royal Navy's official history of the war at sea, shortly after Duff's arrival the Admiralty compiled an "exhaustive survey" of the existing inventory of ASW means and methods. First, "items in the general plan of attacking U-boats wherever they could be found" were reviewed: mines and depth charges, "hunter-killer" submarines, special hydrophone-equipped "hunting patrols," and so forth. Considered separately were ways to give better protection to shipping: more gun-armed merchantmen, more net barrages across the Strait of Dover, and finally, convoys.[81] As the war's official naval historian put it blandly, "Their [i.e., convoys'] position on the list would suffice to show that they were not regarded as of particular importance."[82]

Jellicoe certainly held to this point of view at the time. On 2 November, while still commander in chief of the Grand Fleet and shortly before the fall of the Asquith government, he met with the War Committee, including Lloyd George. According to Hankey, the meeting broached for the first time the subject of convoys.[83] Jellicoe strongly backed the Admiralty's official position that convoying was neither desirable nor feasible.[84] According to one of his admiring biographers, Admiral Reginald Bacon, "Sir John" had studied "the question thoroughly from the Admiralty point of view."[85] His conclusions presumably shared the Admiralty's pessimistic appraisal at the time, that little or nothing had yet or might ever be found to defeat the U-boats conclusively and that therefore "we must for the present be content with palliation."[86]

In his book *The Submarine Peril,* Jellicoe would later highlight the various improvements that were made in the area of offensive ASW countermeasures during his early months as head of the Admiralty. He seems to have particularly taken seriously the deterrent effect of arming merchantmen with guns. According to his own account, of 310 defensively armed ships attacked between 1 January 1916 and 25 January 1917, 236 escaped, sixty-two were sunk by torpedoes, and only twelve were sunk by gunfire. By contrast, only sixty-seven out of 302 unarmed ships escaped. Two hundred five of the victims were sunk by gunfire "or bombs."[87]

Unfortunately, these statistics are somewhat misleading in that the sinkings of armed vessels appear to have been concentrated at the end of the year. *Naval Operations* reports that the number of armed vessels sunk was in fact quite small until August 1916 but that twelve armed merchant ships were sunk in December and another twenty the next month.[88] These numbers are significant and take on a very different meaning than suggested by Jellicoe when it is realized that the total number of British vessels sunk by submarines in December and January was thirty-six each.[89] In other words, 33 percent of ships (twelve out of thirty-six) sunk in December were armed, and a whopping 56 percent (twenty out of thirty-six) in January. Evidently, whatever deterrent value arming merchant vessels might have had before had been largely neutralized by the U-boats' more circumspect approach tactics and more powerful gun armament. In any case, whatever residual deterrent value was left would be rendered null and void once the U-boats' restrictive ROE were lifted and the boats were free to attack without warning. Even while war was still being fought according to the Prize Regulations, the steadily escalating toll that was being exacted portended worse to come. In the words of one German historian, the threat of an unrestricted onslaught hung over the British Isles like the "sword of Damocles."[90]

"The Most Tremendous Undertaking"

The decision to cut the thin thread that held the sword was made on 9 January 1917 at a crown council held at the emperor's residence in Pless, Silesia. The date of 1 February was set as the date for opening the campaign. All shipping, enemy and neutral, including passenger ships, would be liable to attack without warning. The principal war zones included the waters encompassing the British Isles, including the Channel; the western half of the North Sea; and the waters extending four hundred nautical miles from the west coast of France. Also declared a war zone was the entire Mediterranean Sea, with the exceptions of Spanish coastal waters and a lane, twenty nautical miles wide, set aside for Greek steamers. In March, the Barents Sea was added to the list. Further expansions, encompassing broad swaths of water around the Azores and Canary Islands and, eventually, most of the North Atlantic, were declared in November 1917 and January 1918.[91] Over a hundred U-boats stood poised to launch what Scheer labeled "the most tremendous undertaking that the world-war brought in its long train."[92]

The aim was no less than to compel Britain to sue for peace within five to six months. The Germans had done their homework. A team of civilian economic, financial, and maritime experts commissioned by the naval staff had calculated that if the U-boats could sink 600,000 tons of shipping each month, and if 40 percent of neutral shipping could be frightened into staying in port, five months would suffice to reduce the amount of shipping for Britain's supply needs by 39 percent. This, the group predicted, would be an "unacceptable loss."[93] As matters turned out, the basic statistics were sound. Accurate also was the calculation that the United States would likely join Germany's enemies but that it would take eighteen months for its vast resources to be fully mobilized, presumably far too late to rescue the British.[94] The fatal flaw in the calculations concerned certain underlying premises and assumptions—for example, the belief that the British "political system" was incapable of imposing onerous food rationing.[95]

The naval leadership too had its assumptions. Von Holtzendorff was convinced that if his U-boats could dispatch 300,000 to 400,000 tons of shipping to the bottom each month despite the Prize Regulations, it should manage 600,000 tons without those restrictions. The basis of the navy's chief of staff's confidence was the belief that increased U-boat losses due to improved enemy countermeasures would be more than offset by new additions to the order of battle. Implicit in this estimate was the assumption that enemy defensive improvements would be slow and evolutionary—more ships, more mines, etc. No thought seems to have been given to the possibility of a British "breakthrough" solution that might somehow defeat the 600,000-tons-per-month goal. The German navy's propaganda had painted the U-boat as an unbeatable "wonder weapon"; a British countermiracle within the next six months was unimaginable.

Von Holtzendorff's expectations seemed well-founded in the first few months of the unrestricted campaign. In February, worldwide shipping losses climbed to about 500,000 tons, in March to some 540,000 tons, and in April, the allies' worst, over 840,000 tons disappeared.[96] This averaged to just about the 600,000 tons per month the German navy had calculated would be necessary to bring Britain to its knees. The hope that up to 40 percent of neutral shipping would be deterred from continuing to trade with Britain seemed to be borne out as well. In January 1917, the number of port entrances and clearances by neutral vessels over one thousand tons had still been 471 and 832, respectively. The numbers of entrances and clearances in February and March combined fell to 299 and 660, respectively.[97] Since the output of British shipyards was far less than the losses, the only way for the country to make ends meet now was to impose further import restrictions. In February cuts amounting to 500,000 tons a month in commodities ranging from luxury items, such as coffee and silk clothing, to basic foodstuffs and raw factory materials were announced.[98] The supply of basic foodstuffs at this time was estimated to be enough to last six weeks at best.[99]

Notes

1. Sir Julian S. Corbett, *Naval Operations* (London: Longmans, Green, 1921), vol. 2, p. 133.

2. Ibid., p. 18.

3. Robert M. Grant, *U-boats Destroyed: The Effect of Anti-submarine Warfare 1914–1918* (London: Putnam, 1964), p. 20. This number does not include U-boats sunk by decoy trawlers.

4. Günter Krause, *U-Boot Alarm: Zur Geschichte der U-Boot-Abwehr (1914–1945)* (Berlin: Brandenburgische Verlagshaus, 1998), p. 34.

5. Adm. Sir Reginald Bacon, *The Dover Patrol 1915–1917* (London: Hutchinson, 1919), vol. 2, p. 391.

6. Arno Spindler, *Der Krieg zur See 1914–1918: Der Handelskrieg mit U-booten,* vol. 2, *Februar bis September 1915* (Berlin: E. S. Mittler and Son, 1933; trans. Naval War College as *The War at Sea, 1914–1918: The Submarine War on Commerce* [Newport, R.I.: Department of Intelligence and Research, 1934]), p. 31. Even though the nets themselves were not emplaced until much later, merchant vessels and the Germans were led to believe otherwise by a system of warning buoys and lightships. According to Spindler, "They hinted at something that did not exist . . . and the British blockade profited thereby."

7. On the poor performance of British mines, see Bacon, *Dover Patrol 1915–1917,* vol. 1, pp. 69–70; Capt. J. S. Cowie, *Mines, Minelayers and Minelaying* (London: Oxford Univ. Press, 1949), pp. 47–44; and Krause, *U-Boot Alarm,* p. 34.

8. Krause, *U-Boot Alarm,* p. 34.

9. See Bacon, *Dover Patrol 1915–1917,* vol. 1, pp. 24–41.

10. Corbett, *Naval Operations,* vol. 2, p. 283.

11. Spindler reported the U-boats' rerouting via the northern passage doubled the distance they had to travel to their patrol grounds, from 700 to 1,400 miles for a round trip of fourteen days. This left only four days for the U-boat to operate on its assigned patrol station, which no longer included the waters off London. See Spindler, *War at Sea, 1914–1918,* p. 8. Also, Joachim Schröder, *Die U-Boote des Kaisers* (Bonn: Bernard and Graefe Verlag, 2003), p. 120.

12. Krause, *U-Boot Alarm,* p. 52.

13. Schröder, *Die U-Boote des Kaisers,* p. 475. The instructions also urged that if the vessel flew a neutral flag it be replaced with the British colors before opening fire.

14. Memorandum of the Imperial German Government on the Treatment of Armed Merchantmen, 10 February 1916, available at www.lib.byu.edu/~rdh/wwi/1916/merchant .html.

15. Schröder, *Die U-Boote des Kaisers,* p. 166.

16. Paul Kemp, *U-boats Destroyed: German Submarine Losses in the World Wars* (Annapolis, Md.: Naval Institute Press, 1997), pp. 9–59.

17. *Naval-History.net 1997–2010,* www.naval -history.net/WW1NavyBritishQships.htm.

18. Kemp, *U-boats Destroyed,* p. 13.

19. H. G. Wells wrote in the 11 June issue of the *Times* that this war was essentially a "struggle of invention." He called for much greater efforts at enlisting the country's scientific talent. Cited in Willem Hackmann, *Seek & Strike: Sonar, Anti-submarine Warfare and the Royal Navy 1914–54* (London: H.M. Stationery Off., 1984), p. 13.

20. In 1915, the keels for at least seventy-six U-boats of different types were laid. See Eberhard Rössler, *Die Unterseeboote der*

kaiserlichen Marine (Bonn: Bernard and Graefe Verlag, 1997), pp. 70–140.

21. National Archives, Kew, U.K., ADM 116/1430, *Report of the Board,* 1917.

22. Fisher was effectively forced into early retirement in the wake of his increasingly vitriolic disagreement with Winston Churchill—the Admiralty's First Lord and therefore political head—over the conduct of the Dardenelles campaign. See Paul G. Halpern, *A Naval History of World War I* (Annapolis, Md.: Naval Institute Press, 1994), p. 117.

23. The BIR's six sections were Section I, Airships and General Aeronautics; Section II, Submarines and Wireless Telegraphy; Section III, Naval Construction; Section IV, Antiaircraft Equipment; Section V, Ordnance and Ammunition; Section VI, Armament of Aircraft, Bombs, and Bombsights. Hackmann, *Seek & Strike,* p. 18.

24. Ibid. The board was formally abolished in September 1917 and its work moved to the Admiralty's newly established Central Research Establishment. See also ibid., pp. 28–37.

25. Ibid., p. 19.

26. Ibid., pp. 21–26, 45–55.

27. For an account of the Holland investigation and its politics, see ibid., pp. 32–37.

28. National Archives, Kew, U.K., ADM116/1430, *Report on the Present Organisation of the Board of Invention and Research.*

29. It is no accident that World War I coincided with the end of the "great age of amateurs," in which a serving naval officer could "doodle a design" and see it transformed into a real technical invention. See Hubert C. Johnson, "Anglo-American Naval Inventors, 1890–1919: Last of a Breed," *International Journal of Naval History* 1, no. 1 (April 2002).

30. Schröder, *Die U-Boote des Kaisers,* p. 143.

31. Ibid., p. 177.

32. Hermann Bauer, *Als Führer der U-Boote im Weltkriege: Der Eintritt der U-Boot Waffe in die Seekriegsführung* (Leipzig: Koehler and Amelang, 1941), p. 315. Bauer was the U-boats' commander in chief until June 1917.

33. Cited in Schröder, *Die U-Boote des Kaisers,* p. 179. His complete remark was, "Glauben Sie mir, meine Herren, mit Ihrem Ubootskrieg ritzen Sie dem Walfisch nicht die Haut."

34. Ibid., p. 430. Another 143,000 tons in shipping was lost to other forms of enemy action, mainly mines.

35. The British defined "oceangoing ships" as steam vessels of at least 1,600 gross registered tonnage.

36. Dwight R. Messimer, *Find and Destroy: Antisubmarine Warfare in World War I* (Annapolis, Md.: Naval Institute Press, 2001), p. 70.

37. Fayle's official British account of the war against trade reports that thanks to the capture of enemy ships, the total tonnage available in the fall of 1915 was actually greater than at the outbreak of war. C. Ernest Fayle, *History of the Great War: Seaborne Trade* (New York: Longmans, Green, 1923), vol. 2, p. 167.

38. Krause, *U-Boot Alarm,* p. 53.

39. Schröder, *Die U-Boote des Kaisers,* p. 437.

40. Ibid., pp. 427–28.

41. Fayle, *History of the Great War,* vol. 2, p. 167.

42. Ibid. (See Fayle's comment.)

43. Ibid., p. 128.

44. Fayle, *History of the Great War,* vol. 3, table 1, p. 465. Not surprisingly monthly worldwide losses showed a similar rise, from an average of 86,504 tons between January and July to 185,866 and 151,884 tons in August and September, respectively.

45. Fayle, *History of the Great War,* vol. 2, p. 168.

46. Ibid., p. 169.

47. Ibid., p. 177.

48. Ibid., p. 231.

49. Winston S. Churchill, *The World Crisis 1911–1918* (London: Odhams, 1923–27), vol. 2, p. 719. Churchill repeated the numbers as cited by Corbett in *Naval Operations,* vol. 2, pp. 284–85.

50. Churchill, *World Crisis 1911–1918,* pp. 731–32.

51. Schröder, *Die U-Boote des Kaisers,* p. 473.

52. Grey said, "What we want to do is to prevent goods reaching or coming from the enemy country, and that is what we are doing," and "No ships are going through to German ports at all." Ibid., p. 189.

53. Ibid., p. 428.

54. Ibid., p. 191. See also Bauer, *Als Führer der U-Boote im Weltkriege,* p. 347.

55. Schröder, p. 198.

56. Ibid.

57. The Type D depth-charge design and its variants had a TNT charge of up to three hundred pounds. It was preset to explode at either forty or eighty feet and, according to British figures, would destroy a submarine at a range of seventy feet and cause severe damage out to 140 feet. Messimer, *Find and Destroy,* pp. 77–78.

58. Krause, *U-Boot Alarm,* p. 57.

59. Admiral Viscount Jellicoe of Scapa, *The Grand Fleet 1914–16: Its Creation, Development and Work* (London: Cassell, 1919), p. 227.

60. Henry Newbolt, *Naval Operations* (London: Longmans, Green, 1928), vol. 4, pp. 333–37.

61. Andreas Michelsen, *Der U-Bootskrieg 1914–1918* (Leipzig: Hafe and Koehler Verlag, 1942), p. 182. Vice Admiral Michelsen commanded the High Sea Fleet's submarines from June 1917 till the end of the war.

62. Ibid., p. 209.

63. This calculation was made by Newbolt in *Naval Operations,* vol. 4, p. 51.

64. Schröder, *Die U-Boote des Kaisers,* p. 430.

65. Fayle, *History of the Great War,* vol. 3, p. 467.

66. Admiral Scheer, *Germany's High Sea Fleet in the World War* (London: Cassell, 1920), p. 130.

67. Cited in Schröder, *Die U-Boote des Kaisers,* p. 219.

68. The Germans correctly guessed that since few American citizens traveled in the Mediterranean, they could safely continue operations there.

69. Maj. A. C. B. Alexander, *Jutland: A Plea for a General Naval Staff* (London: Hugh Rees, 1923), p. 51. See also John Buchan, *A History of the Great War* (Boston: Houghton Mifflin, 1922), vol. 3, p. 316. Scheer's claim that the High Sea Fleet's guns were critical to the U-boat campaign gives indirect support to the argument, but one suspects that he sought to deflect criticism of "his" High Sea Fleet's relative inactivity during the war.

70. The British lost three battle cruisers and three armored cruisers, as well as eight flotilla leaders and destroyers combined. Casualties, including dead and wounded, were 6,768. The Germans lost one predreadnought battleship, four light cruisers, and five destroyers; their casualties were 3,058. Halpern, *Naval History of World War I,* p. 326.

71. Admiral of the Fleet, the Rt. Hon. Earl Jellicoe, *The Submarine Peril: Admiralty Policy in 1917* (London: Cassell, 1934), p. 24.

72. Krause, *U-Boot Alarm,* p. 54.

73. Scheer, *Germany's High Sea Fleet in the World War,* p. 177.

74. Schröder, *Die U-Boote des Kaisers,* pp. 237–38.

75. Ibid., p. 430.

76. Fayle, *History of the Great War,* vol. 2, pp. 380–81.

77. Lord Hankey, *The Supreme Command 1914–1918* (London: George Allen and Unwin, 1961), vol. 2, p. 643.

78. Cited in Stephen Roskill, *Hankey: Man of Secrets,* vol. 1, *1877–1918* (Annapolis, Md.: Naval Institute Press, 1970), p. 315.

79. Fayle, *History of the Great War,* vol. 2, p. 378.

80. Jellicoe, *Submarine Peril,* p. 35.

81. Newbolt, *Naval Operations,* vol. 4, pp. 325–32.

82. Ibid., p. 332.

83. Hankey, *Supreme Command 1914–1918,* p. 553.

84. Peter Rowland, *David Lloyd George: A Biography* (New York: Macmillan, 1976), pp. 393–94.

85. Admiral Sir R. H. Bacon, *The Life of John Rushworth Earl Jellicoe* (London: Cassell, 1936), p. 352.

86. Ibid., p. 351.

87. Jellicoe, *Submarine Peril,* p. 15. His biographer, Bacon, provides the identical figures. Bacon, *Life of John Rushworth Earl Jellicoe,* p. 353.

88. Newbolt, *Naval Operations,* vol. 4, p. 331.

89. *British Vessels Lost at Sea 1914–18, Section II: Merchant Shipping (Losses)* (Cambridge, U.K.: Patrick Stevens, 1977), pp. 27–31.

90. Schröder, *Die U-Boote des Kaisers,* p. 251.

91. "Sperrgebiete um Europa und Afrika" and "Amerikanische Sperrgebiet." Maps included in Michelsen, *Der U-Bootskrieg 1914–1918.*

92. Scheer, *Germany's High Sea Fleet in the World War,* p. 254.

93. Schröder, *Die U-Boote des Kaisers,* p. 298.

94. Holger H. Herwig, *The Politics of Frustration: The United States in Naval Planning, 1889–1941* (Boston: Little, Brown, 1971), pp. 117–21, 126–28.

95. For a critical review of the thinking underlying Germany's decision to declare unrestricted U-boat war, see Holger H. Herwig, "Total Rhetoric, Limited War: Germany's U-Boat Campaign 1917–1918," *Journal of Military and Strategic Studies* (Spring 1988), available at www.jmss.org/.

96. Sources differ slightly over the tonnage of shipping sunk. For example, Fayle, *History of the Great War,* vol. 3, p. 465, reports losses of 540,006, 593,841, and 881,027 tons in February, March, and April, respectively. Schröder, *Die U-Boote des Kaisers,* p. 430, cites 499,430, 548,817, and 841,118 tons, respectively.

97. Fayle, *History of the Great War,* vol. 3, p. 53.

98. Ibid., p. 63.

99. Krause, *U-Boot Alarm,* p. 59.

CHAPTER THREE

"The Old Theories Have Been Tried and Found Wanting"

The huge British defensive effort so far was clearly a shambles.[1] Writing in his diary on 8 February, Hankey admitted that it looked like "our military effort would so far exhaust us that we cannot maintain our sea power and our economic position." He consoled himself that his country seemed at least to be sinking "a good many submarines."[2] He was wrong. In February, the Germans lost five U-boats, four of which due to enemy action. In March and April another four boats fell victim to mines and other hostile causes.[3] In other words, 1,104 ships were sunk at the cost of nine attackers.

Henry Newbolt quite rightly labeled the U-boats' "power to force unwieldy and disproportionate concentrations of ships" as "most extraordinary."[4] In his chronicle of the war at sea, he summarized the vast arsenal of ASW forces deployed in February 1917:

> In February 1917 about two-thirds of our destroyer strength, and all our submarines, minesweepers and auxiliaries, were engaged in some branch of submarine warfare. . . . In Home waters and the Mediterranean about three thousand destroyer and auxiliary patrol vessels were engaged in combating the submarine menace, either directly or indirectly; so that every German submarine was diverting some twenty-seven craft and their crews from other duties by pinning them to patrol areas and forcing them to spend their time in screening, searching and hunting operations which very rarely ended in success.[5]

The Royal Navy's mainstay strategic scheme for giving inbound and outbound shipping at least a modicum of protection was rapidly unraveling. Involved here was the so-called approach-areas strategy. This protective system had been introduced off the south coast of Ireland in the summer of 1915 but had gradually expanded to three "great cones of approach" in which oceanic shipping converged on Britain's largest ports. The scheme called for inbound shipping to be routed along very thinly patrolled approach routes until it arrived in home waters and could benefit from the more heavily patrolled inshore routes. Outbound shipping followed the reverse procedure. The system worked reasonably well while the U-boats operated near shore; it fell apart when the larger boats sought their prey some two hundred nautical miles farther west, where patrol coverage was weak or nonexistent as the approach routes converged toward the protected inshore lanes.[6] These "danger areas" of some ten to fifteen thousand square miles quickly became death traps from which twenty-five out of every hundred steamers that left Britain in the spring of 1917 failed to return.[7] As the minister of shipping wrote after the war, they had become the "graveyard of British shipping."[8] Even the Admiralty was compelled to admit at the end of March that despite all efforts, the attack had outstripped the defense, with no solution in sight.[9] The implication was obvious: "The end of the war could be fixed with arithmetical precision at no very distant date."[10]

One of Winston Churchill's most memorable phrases of World War II pays tribute to the young men who won the Battle of Britain and thereby arguably saved the country from German invasion. "Never in the field of human conflict," the prime minister declared on 20 August 1940, "was so much owed by so many to so few." With only a slight exaggeration, the same might be said of two relatively junior Royal Navy officers who in World War I "bucked the system" to catalyze the "counterrevolution in military affairs" that halted the slide to seemingly inevitable defeat. Their names have become footnotes at best in most histories of the U-boat campaign, but had it not been for their willingness to question, at considerable risk to their careers, the prevailing assumptions and "facts" about the conduct of the anti-U-boat war, the "final solution" to the U-boat problem—that is, the convoy system—might never have been adopted. The two were Commander (later Admiral Sir) Reginald Henderson and Captain (later Vice Admiral) Kenneth G. B. DeWar. Both worked in the Admiralty, Henderson in the Anti-Submarine Division and DeWar in the Operations Division. It is not clear from the evidence which of the two took the initiative, the problem being in part that their accounts of their respective experiences are curiously similar. In any event, between the two it was discovered, first, that the attrition to British shipping was far greater than the public statistics suggested and, second, that the actual number of oceangoing ships arriving at and sailing from British ports was much smaller than was advertised, making the provision of convoy escorts a much more manageable undertaking than had been claimed by the Admiralty.

The Henderson version of events is the one more often cited. Bits and pieces appear in Lloyd George's and Hankey's memoirs, as well as in the official histories of the war at sea. DeWar's version is found in his own memoirs, *The Navy from Within*.[11] In any event, both officers, finding that the Admiralty itself could not provide reliable statistics about the comings and goings of overseas shipping, reportedly turned to the newly created Ministry of Shipping. Henderson supposedly did so in connection with his responsibility for organizing the "controlled" sailings of the cross-Channel coal trade to France. Practically speaking, these were convoys, but the Admiralty was evidently not quite ready to use that name. For his part, DeWar would write that he needed better statistics to prepare the Admiralty's "Weekly Appreciation" of the U-boat war. According to his account, the Admiralty's Trade Division could tell him only the number and tonnage of ships sunk; customs returns gave him a tabulation of weekly arrivals and sailings.

With the help of Norman Leslie of the Ministry of Shipping, it did not take long to realize that the customs numbers grossly exaggerated the actual number of vessels that called on British ports. "These figures," DeWar wrote later, "had been started as propaganda for the public."[12] For example, the report of 1,800 cross-Channel passages each month involved only about two hundred vessels. DeWar's next Weekly Appreciation, which reported that arrivals and departures of oceangoing ships that week had amounted to only two hundred, was met with two reactions. First, there was disbelief; the First Lord had become so accustomed to hearing the inflated customs returns that he thought DeWar must be using *daily* figures. The second response was bureaucratic. DeWar, according to his own account, had transgressed the rules of the Admiralty, by contacting another ministerial department without proper clearance to do so. In contemporary military terminology, he had failed to "staff" his initiative properly. Punishment came swiftly. Jellicoe ordered his immediate reassignment to a derelict cruiser lying in Colombo harbor, Ceylon. Thanks to his wife's political connections, DeWar succeeded in blocking this.[13]

The story of Henderson's role is very similar. Henderson, according to Lloyd George's autobiography, discovered the "fateful error in accountantship which nearly lost us the War." It was an error, he wrote, that would not have been made by "an ordinary clerk in a shipping office" (a reference to Lloyd's Register) and that could have been avoided with common sense and a "sum in simple addition." Unfortunately, wrote the prime minister, no one on the Board of Admiralty in the spring of 1917 had "possessed this triple qualification."[14] Henderson belonged to the "convoy lobby" of young officers within the Admiralty; the revealing statistics were, in a sense, his last, best chance to undermine the institution's persistent refusal to consider the convoys as either desirable or feasible. As already hinted in DeWar's account, the Admiralty itself was not likely to welcome Henderson's numbers, especially their implication that convoying might be a practical proposition after all: the "real" numbers impugned the "High Admirals'" common sense, and if the statistics strengthened the case for convoying, their strategic wisdom was in question as well.[15] Knowing this, Henderson circumvented the navy's formal chain of command and contacted the political leadership directly. The indications are that he chose Hankey, Lloyd George's éminence grise, as his point of contact. Hankey himself does not mention any such meeting in his autobiography, but his biographer, Stephen Roskill, believed this to be almost certainly the case.[16] There is a possibility also that, perhaps at Hankey's instigation, Henderson went to see Lloyd George directly. The prime minister's autobiography makes no specific mention of such a conversation but makes clear that he met with a number of junior officers who were critical of their superiors' ASW schemes and refusal to consider the convoy option seriously.[17] Jellicoe and his biographer, Admiral Bacon, also mention Lloyd George's penchant for seeking out the opinions of junior officers. Not surprisingly, neither Jellicoe nor Bacon was pleased. "There were apparently certain junior officers who went to, and were received by, Mr. Lloyd George, and who formulated to him ideas for dealing with the submarine menace," Jellicoe wrote. "Personally," he went on, "I had never heard of their proposals," and in any case, it was "strange that they did not ask to see me nor some other officer in authority."[18] Bacon too was dismissive of "some junior officers and laymen" who, in his words, "egged on" the prime minister to force the immediate adoption of the convoy. Fortunately, Bacon reported, Jellicoe "withstood Mr. Lloyd George's visionary ideas until America entered the war."[19]

The admirals' unhappiness is understandable. These junior officers had clearly violated the chain of command; their advocacy outside the Admiralty Board Room of a strategy that was clearly at odds with the agreed strategy smacked of insubordination, if not outright sabotage. The officers' most grievous sin, though, was that by confiding in the country's political leadership they had breached the navy's long and jealously guarded immunity from civilian interference.[20] In the past, both sides had always understood that decisions on how and where to fight belonged to the professional senior officers; the latter had always made it clear that without a free hand they could not be responsible for the conduct of war. In March 1917, at the height of the convoy debate, the navy's long-treasured independence received one of its last hurrahs from the First Lord, Sir Edward Carson. "I advise the country," he declared in a luncheon speech, "to pay no attention to amateur strategists, who are always impatient and always ready for a gamble. We cannot afford to gamble with our fleet. As long as I am at the Admiralty the sailors will have full scope. They will not be interfered with by me and I will not let anyone interfere with them."[21]

Lloyd George himself had honored this tradition during his first few months in office. He had approved the Admiralty's now familiar but largely ineffective countermeasure programs, for two reasons. First, like most of the British public, he underestimated the severity of Britain's condition.[22] Second, being new in office, he was not ready to dispute the professional judgment of "the most famous specialists . . . in the United Kingdom."[23] Consequently, though perhaps not wisely, he allegedly resolved that Jellicoe was to "be given a fair trial."[24]

The Henderson/DeWar numbers ended Jellicoe's "honeymoon" with Lloyd George; the Admiralty's monopoly on decision making was *finis*. The end began on 13 February, when the prime minister invited Carson, Jellicoe, and his ASW chief, Admiral Duff, to 10 Downing Street. Hankey also attended. On the agenda was a memorandum prepared by Hankey advocating the adoption of convoying at the earliest possible date.[25] Hankey has described his proposal as the result of "a brainwave on the subject of anti-submarine warfare" he had had a few days earlier.[26] His biographer speculates as to whether this "brainwave" was perhaps triggered by a meeting with Henderson.[27] The navy's leadership were not yet ready to be convinced, however. Only a month before, Jellicoe had told the War Cabinet that he wanted more decoy ships, as these were "the most effective method of dealing with submarines."[28] As for convoys, the admirals told Lloyd George that merchant ships could not sail in formation, that not enough destroyers were available for escorts, that a convoy would have to sail at the speed of the slowest vessel, and that a group of ships presented a much bigger and more vulnerable target than a vessel traveling alone. The admirals did agree, however, to monitor carefully the results of ongoing trial convoys to France and Norway.[29] Although he had achieved much less than he wanted, Lloyd George was not quite ready yet to bring matters to a head.

Jellicoe, on his part, does not seem to have looked upon the French and Norwegian convoy "experiments" with particularly objective detachment. When at a meeting of the War Cabinet on 23 April Lloyd George again raised the possibility of adopting the convoy system, Jellicoe agreed "to make a further report on the matter" but reminded the prime minister that "the trial" of the Norwegian convoy "had not been altogether successful, two vessels in separate convoys already having been torpedoed and sunk."[30] The First Sea Lord evidently continued to place much more stock in "traditional" weapons (now including American ones)—more destroyers, more patrol vessels, and more aircraft—to patrol danger areas and hunt down U-boats. "Quite obviously," wrote Newbolt, "the First Sea Lord did not then contemplate any fundamental alteration in our entire system of defence."[31]

In his study of the influence of perceptions on policy making, Robert Jervis has noted how people who favor a particular policy usually believe that it is supported by many logically independent reasons. What is interesting about this phenomenon is that from a strictly rational perspective, there is no need to marshal multiple reasons for one's preference—each by itself would suffice. The same holds for people who *oppose* a particular policy. According to Jervis, this tendency toward "overkill" in belief systems marked the Admiralty's resistance against the introduction of convoying.[32]

The reasons given why convoying was neither feasible nor desirable can be summarized as follows. To begin with, it was feared that ships sailing closely together, emitting a massive combined plume of smoke, would be more, not less, likely spotted by a prowling U-boat than would ships steaming singly. It was easy to visualize what would happen next: while the attacker picked off its targets at leisure, the surviving ships would panic, lose formation, and collide in their haste to flee the killing ground. In any case, many naval and merchant marine officers doubted whether a group of ships could sail a tightly controlled zigzag course even when not under attack; more ships might be lost as the result of collisions than of actions of the enemy. In his memoirs Jellicoe acknowledges that this concern turned out "somewhat exaggerated" but asserts that it was based at the time on his consultations with "many" merchant shipmasters.[33] Jellicoe may have had any number of informal conversations of this kind, but the record reports only one official discussion. It took place on 23 February 1917. Ten masters were invited, nine attended. Jellicoe found that all nine much preferred to sail alone rather than in company. They "were quite emphatic" in their opinion, he wrote, that it would be impossible for eight ships, sailing in two columns and at speeds differing by, say, two knots, to keep station two and a half cables (about five hundred yards) apart.[34]

Jellicoe's suggested station-keeping criteria are interesting. They were evidently not based on any "field test" but borrowed from the Grand Fleet. When in cruising forma-tion, the Grand Fleet's battleships were typically organized into four-ship divisions, which, like Jellicoe's suggested convoy, steamed in columns, each ship two and a half cables from the ship ahead and the columns themselves eight cables, or 1,600 yards, apart.[35] Keeping exact station could be difficult even for practiced navy crews. In the event of difficulties (arising from weather or high speed, for example) standing instruc-tions called for ships to increase the distance between them.[36] With this background in mind, the shipmasters' negative reaction to Jellicoe's rather stringent convoy require-ments is not surprising. Perhaps more surprising is that Jellicoe apparently did not take a leaf from the Admiralty's own instructions and ask whether station keeping would be feasible if spacing between ships was greater—perhaps doubled to five cables. More-over, a skeptic could have pointed out that the key reason for the close spacing of war-ships was not relevant to merchant vessels. Tight station keeping was necessary to minimize the time the battle fleet needed to make the transition from cruising to battle formation; there was no such need for a merchant convoy. But then perhaps Jellicoe was not looking for an answer that might "prove" the convoy.[37] Interestingly, when the convoy system was instituted, the typical spacing between ships in column was one thousand yards, and that between columns as much as two thousand yards.[38]

The Admiralty's excessive (as it turned out) estimate of the number of escorts needed to protect a convoy may also have had its roots in Grand Fleet practice. Admiralty opinion at the time had it that escorting forces would have to be twice as numerous as the vessels being escorted.[39] As in the case of the station-keeping issue, this was evi-dently an a priori opinion, resting on neither practical experience with convoy screen-ing nor any form of careful analysis. Instead, the two-to-one relationship in the Grand

Fleet's order of battle between screening forces of light cruisers and destroyers and the screened capital ships seems to have been used as the benchmark.[40]

If the Grand Fleet model for escort requirements indeed formed the basis for the Admiralty's estimate of how many ships would be needed to protect convoys, the consequences were unfortunate. "Not enough destroyers" was constantly cited as a key reason why convoying, however desirable it might be on other grounds (which it was not, in the eyes of most admirals), was infeasible.[41] No one evidently considered that a battle fleet's destroyer screen served an entirely different purpose from a convoy's—the first was there to attack the enemy's battleships with torpedoes and defend its own battleships against enemy torpedo destroyers; the second was designed simply to protect.

When the convoys set sail in 1917, the continued shortage of escort forces compelled much thinner screens than were thought necessary. On paper, and depending on the number of ships involved, a convoy was supposed to be accompanied by at least six destroyers. Instead many convoys had only one escort on much of their route.[42] To everyone's surprise and contrary to the Admiralty's dire forebodings, it turned out that even a few or relatively poorly armed vessels often deterred all but the most intrepid U-boat commanders. Contrary to what may seem common sense, there proved to be no direct relationship between the number of ships in the convoy and the number of escorts needed. Larger convoys did require more escorts, but proportionately fewer than small convoys. That is so because the number of ships needed for a screen is determined by the size of the convoy's perimeter, not the number of ships per se. It has been learned, in fact—though only after analysis many years after the war—that the larger the convoy the safer the ship.[43]

Shipping interests feared that delays and port congestion, and therefore lowered earning power, would be one of convoying's unavoidable consequences. Delays would come in any number of ways. First, many vessels would have to make intermediate voyages from their ports of loading to ports of concentration; there they would have to wait while the convoy was being collected. Next, once the convoy was under way, the faster ships would have to reduce their speed to that of the slowest in the convoy. Finally, there would be more delays when the ships arrived in their ports of discharge, where facilities were not designed to handle the "pulse arrivals" of large groups of ships.[44] An added worry from the point of view of the authorities concerned the effect of the delays on the delivery rate of goods. These were all reasonable and, to a degree, justified arguments. From the perspective of the overall war effort, though, they turned out to be manageable. Even Jellicoe, hardly an optimist, acknowledged that the feared turnaround problem associated with the sudden arrival of large numbers of ships was eventually "enormously decreased."[45] The convoy system did adversely affect delivery rates. No detailed calculations for World War I are available, but the numbers for World War II are presumably representative. It was found then that depending on the route, delivery rates declined by 10 to 14 percent. This must be compared, however, with the cumulative effect on delivery rates of the much higher ship losses among "independents," which was far more serious, at least during World War II.[46]

Many of the war-winning advantages of the convoy system would become evident only after it had been put into practice. Some would be realized only many years afterward, when the raw statistics were finally evaluated with the help of the sophisticated tools of analysis that have collectively become known as operational (or operations) analysis. But in April 1917, the time for prevarication and worry over the real and perceived risks of convoying was rapidly running out. The reality was that even if convoying suffered from all the disadvantages the "High Admirals" claimed, it could produce no worse results than were being obtained by current methods. The problem was—at least according to Lloyd George—that the Admiralty could not admit to the possibility of a solution that fell outside its professional expertise:

> They were like doctors who, whilst they are unable to arrest the ravages of a disease which gradually weakening the resistance of the patient despite all their efforts, are suddenly confronted with a new, unexpected and grave complication. They go about with gloomy mien and despondent hearts. Their reports are full of despair. It is clear that they think the case is now hopeless. All the same, their only advice is to persist in the application of the same treatment. Any other suggestion is vetoed. Their professional honour is involved in not accepting remedies which they have already refused to consider. What makes it difficult to persuade them to try an obvious cure is that it had been urged upon them by civilians and turned down by the experts with scorn and derision.[47]

Notes

1. Adm. Sir Reginald Bacon, *The Dover Patrol 1915–1917* (London: Hutchinson, 1919), vol 2, p. 114.

2. Stephen Roskill, *Hankey: Man of Secrets,* vol. 1, *1877–1918* (Annapolis, Md.: Naval Institute Press, 1970), p. 355.

3. Robert M. Grant, *U-boats Destroyed: The Effect of Anti-submarine Warfare 1914–1918* (London: Putnam, 1964), pp. 23–26.

4. Henry Newbolt, *Naval Operations* (London: Longmans, Green, 1928), vol. 4, p. 347.

5. Ibid., pp. 347–48.

6. C. Ernest Fayle, *History of the Great War: Seaborne Trade* (New York: Longmans, Green, 1923), vol. 3, pp. 90–91.

7. Sir Norman Leslie, "The Convoy System in 1917–18: Convoy and Transportation during the War," in *The Naval Review 1919,* ed. Earl Brassey and John Leyland (London: William Clowes and Sons, 1919), p. 148. Norman Leslie, later Sir Norman, headed up the Ministry of Shipping in 1917–18.

8. Ibid., p. 149.

9. Newbolt, *Naval Operations,* vol. 4, p. 371.

10. Leslie, "Convoy System in 1917–18," p. 148.

11. Vice Adm. K. G. B. DeWar, *The Navy from Within* (London: Victor Gollancz, 1939).

12. Ibid., p. 216.

13. Ibid. DeWar blamed Admiralty disapproval of his habit of interpreting, not just "writing up," current operations for what he thought

was a disciplinary reprisal. DeWar wrote a letter to Herbert Lewis, a close friend of Lloyd George and asked him to intervene. It worked, for within days his ignominious reassignment was canceled.

14. David Lloyd George, *War Memoirs* (London: Ivor Nicholson and Watson, 1934), vol. 3, p. 1146.

15. "High Admirals" is how Lloyd George labeled the Admiralty's convoy opponents.

16. Roskill, *Hankey,* vol. 1, pp. 357–58.

17. Lloyd George, *War Memoirs,* p. 1173.

18. Admiral of the Fleet, the Rt. Hon. Earl Jellicoe, *The Submarine Peril: Admiralty Policy in 1917* (London: Cassell, 1934), pp. 36–37.

19. Adm. Sir R. H. Bacon, *The Life of John Rushworth Earl Jellicoe* (London: Cassell, 1936), pp. 354, 369.

20. The careers of both officers survived, indeed thrived. Henderson became a full admiral, DeWar a vice admiral. One suspects that long and illustrious family pedigrees in both cases helped.

21. Cited in Peter Rowland, *David Lloyd George: A Biography* (New York: Macmillan, 1976), p. 397.

22. Ibid., p. 396.

23. Lloyd George, *War Memoirs,* p. 1149.

24. Ibid., p. 1150.

25. Ibid., pp. 1151–55. Also, Lord Hankey, *The Supreme Command 1914–1918* (London: George Allen and Unwin, 1961), vol. 2, pp. 645–48.

26. Ibid., p. 645.

27. Roskill, *Hankey,* vol. 1, p. 356.

28. National Archives, Kew, U.K., CAB 23/1, *War Cabinet Papers December 9, 1916 to February 28, 1917,* "Minutes of a Meeting of the War Cabinet Held at 10 Downing Street on Thursday, January 11, 1917 at 5 PM. The CAB files at Kew contain the War Cabinet papers.

29. Lloyd George, *War Memoirs,* p. 1155. The Norwegian convoy "experiment" was begun in early April on the initiative of the commander of the Grand Fleet, Admiral Beatty. Beatty had come strongly around to the opinion at this time that though success was far from guaranteed, continuous convoying

"must be better than a system which permits 9 vessels being sunk in a very small area in the course of six days." Beatty, letter to First Lord of the Admiralty, 30 April 1917, cited in Rear Adm. W. S. Chalmers, *The Life and Letters of David Beatty* (London: Hodder and Stoughton, 1951), p. 448.

30. National Archives, Kew, U.K., CAB 23/2, *War Cabinet Papers March 1st 1917 to May 30th, 1917,* "Minutes of the Meeting of the War Cabinet Held at 10 Downing Street on April 23, 1917."

31. Newbolt, *Naval Operations,* vol. 4, p. 380.

32. Robert Jervis, *Perception and Misperception in International Politics* (Princeton, N.J.: Princeton Univ. Press, 1976), pp. 128, 134.

33. Jellicoe, *Submarine Peril,* pp. 98–99.

34. National Archives, Kew, U.K., ADM137/2753 Trade Division, Naval Staff, "Meetings Held at the Admiralty on 23rd February, 1917 Regarding the Practicality of Convoys."

35. See John Irving, *The Smoke Screen of Jutland* (New York: David McKay, 1967), p. 30.

36. See Admiralty, Naval Staff, Tactical Section, O.U.5243, *Instructions for Tactical and Strategical Exercises* January 1921, p. 8, available at www.gwpda.org/naval/admtsx/01.htm.

37. Lloyd George seems to have suspected as much. According to his memoirs, the meeting took place without Jellicoe's having consulted the Ministry of Shipping. "It was highly probable," Lloyd George wrote, "that the form in which Admiral Jellicoe put the question might make the seamen fear that they could never carry out properly the station keeping and joint manoeuvring that membership of a convoy demanded." Lloyd George, *War Memoirs,* pp. 1157–58.

38. Günter Krause, *U-Boot Alarm: Zur Geschichte der U-Boot-Abwehr (1914–1945)* (Berlin: Brandenburgische Verlagshaus, 1998), p. 68.

39. Newbolt, *Naval Operations,* vol. 4, p. 383.

40. The Grand Fleet met the Germans at Jutland with thirty-seven battleships and battle cruisers, screened by a total of eighty destroyers.

41. See, for example, Jellicoe, *Submarine Peril,* pp. 112–16.

42. Eric J. Grove, ed., *The Defeat of the Enemy Attack on Shipping 1939–1945* (Aldershot,

U.K.: Ashgate for the Navy Records Society, 1997), p. 10 and table 5. This is a revised edition of the Royal Navy's Naval Historical Section's *Naval Staff History,* vols. 1A and 1B, first completed in 1957. Its principal author was Lt. Cdr. D. W. Waters, RN. Despite its title, the book contains some valuable data on the U-boat campaign of World War I.

43. Ibid., p. 37. Waters, who was largely responsible for this finding, formulated and quantified the "operational law" that the risk of being attacked to a ship in convoy varies inversely as the size of the convoy.

44. See Fayle, *History of the Great War,* vol. 3, pp. 97–98.

45. Jellicoe, *Submarine Peril,* p. 97.

46. Grove, *Defeat of the Enemy Attack on Shipping 1939–1945,* pp. 308–10.

47. Lloyd George, *War Memoirs,* pp. 1148–49.

CHAPTER FOUR

"We Run a Great Risk of Losing the War"

On the day, 10 April 1917, on which Sims made "the all-important discovery . . . that Britain did *not* control the seas," losses at sea were relatively light.[1] Three ships were torpedoed, but only two sank. At this point, though, few among Britain's political and military leadership doubted that the country was close to economic and military-strategic disaster. In a strong memorandum dated 29 March, Hankey urged "the most drastic measures," including "switch shipping from moving ammunition to bringing wheat from the United States and Canada."[2] He effectively called for scaling back the war effort to prevent a national food crisis. The gravity of the food crisis became painfully evident in the War Cabinet's decision two days afterward to extend rationing to the trenches—the soldiers would have one potato-less day and fewer potatoes the other six days.[3] The hemorrhage of allied and neutral trading fleets meanwhile continued to out-pace the completion of replacement shipping and the turnaround time for ships brought in for repair. Chances were that the one British ship that managed to escape destruction on the day of Sims's visit had either been so damaged that it had to be writ-ten off or, if not, would not go back to sea for five months. The fact was that for every five ships sunk worldwide, a sixth was damaged; thus, during the first half of 1917, a total of 770,000 tons of shipping were damaged. About 50 percent of the damaged ves-sels were beyond repair and could be considered permanently lost.[4] According to one report, the other 50 percent required an average repair time of four months per ship and a fifth month to return to service.[5] In other words, if the Germans were correct in their calculation that it would take five to six months to bring Britain to its knees, dam-aging a ship had about the same effect as sinking it.

The three weeks after the Jellicoe-Sims meeting proved to be decisive in setting in motion the *strategic* solution that ultimately defeated the U-boat. When he met with Sims, Jellicoe was still giving the Admiralty's stock answer when it came to convoys—not enough destroyers, problems with station keeping, etc.[6] But in the undramatic words of the author of *History of the Great War: Seaborne Trade*, the "unprecedented losses suffered during the last fortnight of April, especially in the approach areas, greatly strengthened the hands of those who advocated the general introduction of the convoy system."[7] Lloyd George's hand was strengthened in particular when he found on a visit to the Grand Fleet on 13 April that its commander, Admiral Beatty, strongly supported convoying. He had also learned that Sims backed the idea.

The War Cabinet, including Jellicoe, met again on 23 April. The First Sea Lord gave a bleak report, "The Submarine and Food Supply." Again, the Admiralty could offer no solutions other than to build up the country's supply. Jellicoe also proposed the construction of lots of small cargo ships, which "would be more immune from attack," as well as a handful of very large, "unsinkable" vessels.[8] Lloyd George reminded him that both Beatty and Sims favored the convoy option. The message must have been clear: the convoy idea was no longer just a will-o'-the-wisp, the idea of a handful of civilians and junior naval officers; it now had the backing of Britain's most senior fleet commander as well as the senior naval representative of Britain's new ally. Jellicoe agreed to "make a further report on the matter," but Lloyd George was evidently less than convinced that this was not another stalling tactic.[9] His assessment, as reported in his autobiography, was that it "was clear that the Admiralty did not intend to take any effective steps in the direction of convoying."[10] Two days later, on 25 April, he received War Cabinet approval to visit the Admiralty on 30 April in order to, in his own words, "take peremptory action on the question of convoys."[11]

The Admiralty knew what was coming. Before placing the matter before the War Cabinet, Lloyd George had informed the First Lord, Edward Carson, of his plan. Matters must have been rather hectic during the next few days. On 26 April, the head of the Admiralty's Anti-Submarine Division, Admiral Duff, gave Jellicoe a memorandum arguing that, thanks in part to the American entry into the war, the time had come to start an ocean convoy system.[12] Jellicoe approved it the next day, so that when the prime minister made his entry into the Admiralty Board Room on 30 April, he found his task, in Hankey's words, "greatly simplified."[13] The Admiralty set up a Convoy Committee to take charge of organizing the system, and the first, experimental convoys, one from Gibraltar and the other from Hampton Roads, set sail on 10 and 24 May, respectively.[14] By September, the system was in "full swing" for the Atlantic and Gibraltar trade. Notably excluded until mid-1918, ostensibly for a lack of escorts, was the Mediterranean.[15]

The Reluctant Counterrevolutionaries

Historians are at odds still over the dynamics of the Admiralty's late and sudden conversion to the convoy system. The most dramatic version of events in the Admiralty Board Room on 30 April has been passed on by Lloyd George's close friend Sir Max Aitken (later Lord Beaverbrook). In his story, the Prime Minister descended upon the Admiralty and seated himself in the First Lord's chair. This was possibly an unprecedented action. It was well within the powers and competence of the Prime Minister; yet there may be no parallels in our history. For one afternoon the Prime Minister took over the full reins of Government from the head of a major department of state. . . . The meeting was a minor triumph for the Prime Minister. . . . Lloyd George had staged a deliberate encounter with the Naval High Command, and had emerged triumphant.[16]

Most later commentators have doubted Beaverbrook's account of events. Hankey, who attended the meeting, makes no mention of the implied drama. John Terraine believes that the story is "good stuff for the port and brandy or the gossip columns, but for nothing else." The decision to convoy, he writes, had been made three days earlier.[17] Lloyd George's own biographer claims that when the prime minister arrived, there had already been an "eleventh-hour conversion on the subject of convoys" and that the visit turned out to be an "amicable affair."[18] Curiously, Jellicoe's biographer, Admiral Bacon, has written that according to Admiral Duff, who was present at the meeting, "it was anti-submarine work and not convoy that was discussed" and that "the interview in no way affected the introduction of the convoy system."[19] What matters, of course, are not the particulars of Lloyd George's visit but whether the prime minster was the key to the convoy decision or merely wanted to place his political imprimatur on a decision that had already been made. The answer touches on the debate of more recent years on whether military innovation tends to come from within the military or mostly occurs under the prodding of civilians.[20]

Today, many decades after the events of April 1917, opinions remain sharply divided. The Admiralty's defenders naturally enough insist that the decision was the Admiralty's. It had been admittedly slow in coming, but this was justified by the need for a deliberate and careful evaluation of the risks involved. Such an evaluation demanded facts, not the "opinions of amateurs."[21] The "facts" became available with the successful results of six weeks of "controlled sailings" for the French coal trade. Another key "fact" was the American entry into the war and the prospect of U.S. Navy destroyers for escort duty. According to Bacon, had Jellicoe given in to Lloyd George's pressure and "rush[ed] the matter, we might well have incurred a disaster, or a series of disasters, which might have led to the condemnation of the convoy system."[22] A similar opinion was voiced by, not surprisingly, Jellicoe's First Lord, Edward Carson. In a published interview after the war, Carson denounced Lloyd George's claim of Jellicoe's opposition to convoy as "the biggest lie ever told." Jellicoe had not opposed the convoy system but "required time to organize it."[23] Other, more recent historians also believe that Lloyd George's showdown with the Admiralty was largely an empty gesture. Paul Halpern is one of those, arguing that the crucial decision on convoys had already been made and was not forced on a reluctant Admiralty on that day.[24] Another is John Terraine. He approvingly cites the observation by Royal Air Force historian Sir Maurice Dean that "it is seldom wrong for governments to adopt a cautious approach, especially in military or commercial matters."[25] Terraine goes on to recite the Admiralty's uncertainties at the time; these men were not hostile to change and innovation as such, but "until 1915, everything about [submarine warfare] was new; there was no previous experience for guidance."[26] By April 1917, Terraine would have us believe, the members of the Admiralty had collected the necessary experience, "on their own initiative," to undertake convoying.[27]

Others have viewed the Admiralty's acceptance of convoying as reluctant at best. The historian A. J. P. Taylor is perhaps the best-known spokesman on this side of the argument. He claims that Lloyd George gave the "formal order" that convoys be instituted.[28] Not surprisingly, Lloyd George himself takes full credit for putting the Admiralty, as he had it, "in a chastened mood."[29] Then there is Captain DeWar's judgment:

> In deciding between Mr. Lloyd George and the Official History, one must be guided by the nature of the evidence on both sides. The case for the prosecution is strongly supported by documentary evidence, written at the time, whereas that for the defence, credits the naval authorities with opinions and intentions which they only expressed when the war was over. The idea that they were really in favour of convoy, and only awaited a favourable opportunity to introduce it, is neither borne out by the facts nor by their own memoranda. The written word stands out and cannot be erased.[30]

The evidence is mostly circumstantial, but it is difficult to avoid the conclusion that DeWar's assessment is probably closest to the truth. Strictly speaking, Lloyd George did not "order" the Admiralty to institute the convoy system, and again strictly speaking, Jellicoe was ready to go ahead with a convoy scheme when the prime minister called on him. This said, though, it is all but impossible to conclude that the rapidity of the Admiralty's conversion—and a conversion it was—was the result largely of growing pressure from 10 Downing Street. It has been suggested by some authors that Lloyd George was prepared to fire Jellicoe and the navy's political head, Edward Carson, had they again postponed a decision (both were replaced anyway later in the year).[31] Be that as it may, the argument by some of the Admiralty's apologists, including Jellicoe himself, that it had kept convoying under consideration all along and was merely waiting prudently for certain conditions to be met lacks conviction.[32] None of the surviving Admiralty memorandums or minute sheets in the archives hints at any consideration of convoying as a serious option. If there had been any prior to the spring of 1917, when the necessary conditions were supposedly met, it could reasonably be expected that the Admiralty would have by then laid the foundation for carrying out the system if and when activated—convoy marshalling points, routing schedules and schemes, and so forth. But none of the organizational work started until after the Convoy Committee was formed in May 1917. The most likely scenario is that the navy's leadership truly believed that convoying was a "nonstarter" and then readily found facts and judgments in support of its view, thereby reinforcing its bias.

One of those "facts" was, of course, the shortage of escorts, destroyers and otherwise. Jellicoe and others have claimed that the Admiralty's timing of the convoy decision made perfect sense in light of the prospect of American assistance. Yet the U.S. Navy's contribution to the convoy system was quite small compared with that of the British. For example, according to a report prepared by Sims's headquarters in London in the summer of 1918, U.S. Navy forces engaged in antisubmarine operations in British and eastern Atlantic waters at the time amounted to less than 5 percent of the British contribution. Seventy percent of all transatlantic convoys were escorted by British destroyers, 27 percent by American warships.[33] It should be added also that even though the vast majority of the U.S. destroyers on escort duty were committed to protecting the troop convoys that brought the American Expeditionary Force (AEF) to Europe, much of the escort load fell on British destroyers.[34] In fact, an internal Admiralty memorandum prepared for the First Lord on the eve of a visit with U.S. Navy officials in Washington, D.C., stressed that the American entry into the war had actually put *more* strain on British ASW resources. The document is worth quoting, in part for what it reveals about the persisting attitude toward convoying as a misuse of destroyers at the expense of their "proper" purpose, hunting U-boats:

> When the U.S. came into the war the immediate result—and a very welcome result—was the addition of their destroyers to European waters. As the American Army began to appear in France, however, . . . instead of the U.S. advent into the war causing a net augmentation to the Naval Forces of the Alliance, the demands for safeguarding American seaborne traffic increased so enormously that, looking at the matter purely from a Naval point of view, they have become a tax on the Alliance. That tax has entirely fallen upon the British with the result that we have had to utilize essential forces, intended for hunting the submarine, in order to escort the American supplies across the seas; and although it was a quite unavoidable development, the figures of enemy submarines sunk and submarines in commission at the present moment are a striking commentary on this subject.[35]

In terms of sheer numbers, there never was a dearth of *potential* British and allied escorts. The problem was that even as the convoy system came into full bloom, most escort-capable ships were still committed to wasteful hunt-and-kill and "protected lane" patrols. According to one source, only 257 out of a fleetwide total of 5,018 allied warships, or 5.1 percent, were committed to escort duties.[36] It is tempting to speculate that the Admiralty seized on the prospect of American destroyers as a way to preserve its professional self-esteem in agreeing to a decision it knew at this point would be made with or without it.

"It Is the Convoy System Which Baulked Germany"

On 13 October 1918, with the armies of the Central Powers in collapse and final allied victory around the corner, the Admiralty's First Lord told American newspaper reporters that it was the convoy system that had "baulked Germany when she adopted avowedly the inhuman and ruthless method of submarine warfare considered inconceivable and contrary to all the noble traditions of the sea before the war."[37] No one since has disagreed that the convoy system was the key to defeating the revolutionary changes in sea warfare wrought by the submarine. It was a success by any measure, the most important one being, of course, the minimization of losses of ships and cargoes. Surprisingly, perhaps—or so it seemed at first—escorts on convoy screens also turned out to be more productive U-boat killers than their counterparts on dedicated seek-and-destroy patrols. To be sure, the effectiveness of the convoy "antidote" did not become obvious until the spring of 1918. Until then, the U-boats continued to sink a monthly average of nearly 400,000 tons. Even this number underestimates the actual scale of continuing losses, for it does not include an average monthly loss of forty thousand tons due to irreparable damage or another thirty thousand due to marine casualties. Meanwhile, worldwide production of new shipping managed to compensate for only half of the losses.[38] The Admiralty therefore had good reason in the summer of 1917 to present the War Cabinet with a rather gloomy prognosis. With a projected monthly loss rate of 650,000 tons and a national shipbuilding capacity that replaced only a fifth of this number each month, the country was, in the words of an Admiralty memorandum, in a "very serious position." The submarine campaign would not likely force Britain to stop the war, but this could only be guaranteed "if America puts forth her utmost effort."[39] It was only starting in April 1918 that monthly losses consistently fell below 300,000 tons, and it was only in May that Lloyd George could confidently announce that although the U-boat continued to be a threat, it was no longer a danger.[40]

The statistics of the convoy system's success are well known. Out of nearly eighty-four thousand ships convoyed between February 1917 and October 1918, 257 were sunk, for a loss rate of 0.30 percent. During the same period, 1,500 independents were lost, for a loss rate of 5.93 percent. Put in another way, 85.5 percent of the losses suffered came from independents.[41] On the "offensive" side of the ledger, convoy escorts were responsible for sinking twenty-four out of the forty U-boats sunk by surface vessels during the last fifteen months of the war. Hunting patrols accounted for one, with the balance of fifteen being the work of ships patrolling protected lanes.[42] Putting these two sets of figures together—ships lost versus U-boats sunk—Arthur J. Marder has calculated an exchange rate of 19 : 1 for convoyed ships and 140 : 1 for independents. Escorts were the responsible "killers" in the first case, hunting forces and standing patrols in the second. Marder is fully justified in claiming that these figures fully dispel any question about the comparative effectiveness of convoying.[43]

The reason for the convoy's success is far less to be found in the defensive capacity of its screen of escorts (which, it must be remembered, still did not have the ability to detect an underwater enemy) than in the convoy's ability to, for practical purposes, *disappear*. Depending on its size, a convoy might occupy an area from four to ten square miles—

seemingly, in Admiral Sims's words, "about as desirable a target as the submarine could have desired."[44] In truth, and contrary to expectations, a moving ten-square-mile rectangle somewhere among the millions of square miles of the ocean amounts to a very small target. Put differently, the probability of a submarine encountering at least one out of, say, forty ships sailing independently is much higher than its chance of falling upon a forty-ship convoy. Admiral Sims wrote that, also contrary to the popular perception, the convoy and its destroyer screen constituted an *offensive* system, one that compelled the U-boats to fight for every ship they meant to attack.[45] The U-boats operated singly (experimental operations with coordinated pairs were begun in late 1917), which meant that if a convoy was sighted, a boat rarely had a chance to complete more than one attack. This explains why, out of the hundreds of convoys, involving some ninety-five thousand vessels that were attacked by U-boats, only 393 ships were sunk.[46]

If the convoy system reversed the offense/defense balance by forcing the U-boat to put itself in harm's way, it also served to overturn the balance between "hide" and "seek." That is, by "emptying" the seas of hundreds of defenseless merchantmen scattered everywhere, the convoy organizers had shifted the burden of finding the enemy away from the ASW defender and onto the attacking submarine.[47] Karl Dönitz, who would lead the U-boats' second battle of the Atlantic in World War II but was a young U-boat commander in 1918, noted that the "oceans at once became bare and empty."[48] Empirical support for this observation lies in that fact, for example, that of the 219 convoys that crossed the Atlantic between October and December 1917, only thirty-nine were spotted.[49]

Thanks to its excellent radio-intercept organization, the Admiralty ensured that the oceans were even emptier than they would have been "naturally." Convoying, unlike U-boat hunting, lent itself admirably to the work of the U-boat-tracking section that had been set up in "Room 40," the Admiralty's intelligence division. As has already been noted, throughout the war the Admiralty had quite reliable intelligence about the general whereabouts and comings and goings of the U-boats. The problem was that the information was rarely accurate and current enough to be useful at the tactical level of submarine hunting. But it was perfectly adequate to alert an incoming convoy and divert it away from an *area* of suspected submarine concentration. It had been impossible to warn ships sailing independently, not only because no one ashore could know from one day to the next where every vessel was, but also because many older ships still had no wireless.[50] The convoy system, on the other hand, gave naval planners the means to fuse U-boat intelligence with complete "situational awareness" about the location of friendly shipping. As a result, wrote a postwar Admiralty monograph, "for the first time one could see the latest information as to enemy submarines side by side with the track of a convoy, and as the [convoy] Commodore's ship was always equipped with wireless, it was possible at once to divert a convoy from a dangerous area."[51]

There remains today a minor debate of sorts as to what exactly made the convoy so successful: was it the ring of defensive escorts, which, even if it did not sink U-boats, had a deterrent effect or made attacks more difficult, or was it evasive routine? Patrick Beesly admits it is impossible to calculate how many ships were saved due to rerouting but believes the numbers to have been significant.[52] Sims was more certain that evasive routing was the key to the convoy's success. In *The Victory at Sea* he goes so far as to point out "the interesting fact that, even had there been no destroyer escort, the convoy itself would have formed a great protection to merchant shipping."[53] Elsewhere, he is quoted as declaring, "History will show, when all the facts are known, that more shipping was saved through . . . keeping track of submarines and routing ships clear of them than by any other single measure."[54] It is curious that this particular benefit had not been anticipated. After all, one of the biggest handicaps of fleet commanders in the past had always been the difficulty of *finding* the enemy fleet, especially when it did not want to be found.

Even with the convoy system in full operation and with growing evidence that it worked, allied naval planners continued to pursue a variety of "offensive" schemes. Two of the more dramatic ones were the Zeebrugge blocking operation and the great "Northern Barrage." The former, carried out in April 1918, was aimed at bottling up the Flanders U-boat flotilla by barricading the Belgian ports of Zeebrugge and Ostend. The Ostend portion of the assault was an unequivocal failure. The Zeebrugge portion, which involved the sinking of three old cruisers filled with concrete, was hailed as a tremendous victory; eight Victoria Crosses were awarded. In truth, a few weeks after the attack British intelligence knew that U-boat traffic had not been stopped. According to Marder, the operation's strategic effect was "almost nil, since nothing material was in fact achieved."[55]

The Northern (or North Sea) Barrage was the U.S. Navy Department's favorite ASW project. Approved by the allies in September 1917, it involved mining the 240 miles separating the Orkney Islands from the Norwegian coast. A huge Anglo-American fleet went to work six months later, depositing the first of 100,000 mines (the original plan called for twice that number). In the event, about seventy thousand mines were laid; as far as is known, four to six U-boats were sunk and a few more damaged.[56] Ironically, more allied minelaying ships than that were sunk or damaged due to the tendency of the mines to explode prematurely. The war ended before the barrier was completed, so it is difficult to offer a final verdict on its effectiveness. The fact that it was created at all, though, is indicative of the lukewarm acceptance by the Admiralty (and the Americans, for the matter) of the convoy system. Marder approvingly cites the Royal Navy's historian of World War II, Captain S. W. Roskill, on this point:

> Even if the ready acceptance of the original proposal [for the Northern Barrage] can, at any rate, be explained by the fact that, at the time, the convoy strategy had not yet fully proved itself, its execution was continued long after the success of the ancient principle was beyond all doubt. Indeed the whole idea of the Northern barrage underlines the lack of the Admiralty's faith in the strategy of convoy and escort.[57]

Notes

1. Rear Adm. William Sowden Sims, *The Victory at Sea* (Garden City, N.Y.: Doubleday, Page, 1921), p. 21 [emphasis in the original].

2. National Archives, Kew, U.K., CAB 21/95, Hankey to PM in minute sheet, 29 March 1917, "Immediate Measures to Be Taken regarding the Food Shipping Problem."

3. National Archives, Kew, U.K., CAB 23/2, *War Cabinet Papers, March 1st, 1917, to May 30th, 1917*. At the time, there were already two meatless and two potato-less days in the public eating facilities in Britain.

4. National Archives, Kew, U.K., CAB23/2, Minutes of a Meeting of the War Cabinet Held at 10 Downing St. on August 2, 1917, Admiralty memorandum, "The Submarine Campaign."

5. National Archives, Kew, U.K., ADM 116/1807, Private Correspondence of Sir Eric Geddes, First Lord of the Admiralty 1917–1919, vol. 4, "Report by Director of Statistics, Admiralty, May 21, 1918."

6. Michael Simpson, ed., *Anglo-American Naval Relations 1917–1919* (Aldershot, U.K.: Gower for the Navy Records Society, 1991), pp. 25, 40–41.

7. C. Ernest Fayle, *History of the Great War: Seaborne Trade* (New York: Longmans, Green, 1923), vol. 3, p. 100.

8. National Archives, Kew, U.K., CAB 23/2, Minutes of a Meeting of the War Cabinet Held at 10 Downing St. on April 23, 1917, Admiralty report, "The Submarine and Food Supply."

9. Ibid.

10. David Lloyd George, *War Memoirs* (London: Ivor Nicholson and Watson, 1934), vol. 3, p. 1162.

11. Ibid.

12. Admiral of the Fleet, the Rt. Hon. Earl Jellicoe, *The Submarine Peril: Admiralty Policy in 1917* (London: Cassell, 1934), p. 124.

13. Lord Hankey, *The Supreme Command 1914–1918* (London: George Allen and Unwin, 1961), vol. 2, p. 651.

14. The Convoy Committee's membership included four Royal Navy officers and Leslie of the Ministry of Shipping. It is interesting that none of the officers ranked higher than captain.

15. Fayle, *History of the Great War,* vol. 3, pp. 141–42.

16. Lord Beaverbrook, *Men and Power* (London: Hutchinson, 1956), pp. 155–56, cited in John Terraine, *The U-boat Wars 1916–1945* (New York: Henry Holt, 1989), p. 59.

17. Terraine, *U-boat Wars 1916–1945,* p. 59.

18. Peter Rowland, *David Lloyd George: A Biography* (New York: Macmillan, 1976), p. 398.

19. Adm. Sir R. H. Bacon, *The Life of John Rushworth Earl Jellicoe* (London: Cassell, 1936), p. 360.

20. The innovation-from-within theory has been advanced most cogently by Stephen Rosen, *Winning the Next War* (Ithaca, N.Y.: Cornell Univ. Press, 1991). The importance of civilian intervention is highlighted by Barry R. Posen, *The Sources of Military Doctrine: France, Britain, and Germany between the World Wars* (Ithaca, N.Y.: Cornell Univ. Press, 1984).

21. "Opinions of amateurs" is the phrase used by a Royal Navy officer who sat in on Jellicoe's meeting with the captains of merchant ships, cited in Bacon, *Life of John Rushworth Earl Jellicoe,* p. 355.

22. Ibid., p. 361.

23. Cited in ibid., p. 389.

24. Paul G. Halpern, *A Naval History of World War I* (Annapolis, Md.: Naval Institute Press, 1994), p. 361.

25. Terraine, *U-boat Wars 1916–1945*, p. 58.

26. Ibid.

27. Ibid., p. 59.

28. A. J. P. Taylor, *English History, 1914–1945* (Harmondsworth, U.K.: Penguin Books, 1970), pp. 121–24.

29. Lloyd George, *War Memoirs*, vol. 3, p. 1163.

30. Vice Adm. K. G. B. DeWar, *The Navy from Within* (London: Victor Gollancz, 1939), pp. 220–21.

31. Joachim Schröder, *Die U-Boote des Kaisers* (Bonn: Bernard and Graefe Verlag, 2003), p. 368.

32. It is interesting to note that the Royal Navy's official website refers to Jellicoe as having opposed and implemented convoying; see www.royal-navy.mod.uk/statis/pages/3523 .html.

33. Intelligence Section, U.S. Naval Headquarters, London, "A Brief Summary of United States Navy Activities in European Waters with an Outline of the Organization of Admiral Sims's Headquarters," memorandum, 3 August 1918, cited in Simpson, *Anglo-American Naval Relations 1917–1919*, pp. 171–74.

34. For example, in the summer of 1918 British destroyers escorted roughly 62 percent of U.S. troops arriving in England. Ibid., p. 173.

35. National Archives, Kew, U.K., ADM 116/1189, *Private Correspondence of Sir Eric Geddes, First Lord of the Admiralty 1917–1919*, vol. 6, "Notes for Guidance as to the Line to Be Adopted in Conference with U.S. Navy Department and in Informal Discussions," undated.

36. Günter Krause, *U-Boot Alarm: Zur Geschichte der U-Boot-Abwehr (1914–1945)* (Berlin: Brandenburgische Verlagshaus, 1998), p. 72. See also Vice Adm. Sir Peter Gretton, "The U-boat Campaign in Two World Wars," in *Naval Warfare in the Twentieth Century, 1900–1945: Essays in Honour of Arthur Marder*, ed. G. Jordan (London: Croom Helm, 1977), pp. 130–34. In August 1917, almost three thousand vessels were committed to various shipping-protection duties, two hundred perhaps of which were committed to convoy escort duties. The figure of three thousand is taken from National Archives, Kew, U.K., CAB 23/2, *War Cabinet Papers, June 5th, 1917 to August 30th, 1917*, Minutes of a Meeting of the War Cabinet on August 2, 1917, Admiralty memorandum on "The Submarine Campaign." The estimate that fewer than two hundred ships were dedicated to convoy escorting is based on Jellicoe's data in Jellicoe, *Submarine Peril*, pp. 162–63. The Royal Navy's staff study reports that ninety-one destroyers and other vessels were available for ocean convoys in July 1917. The maximum number was reached in April 1918, when 195 were available; Eric J. Grove, ed., *The Defeat of the Enemy Attack on Shipping 1939–1945* (Aldershot, U.K.: Ashgate for the Navy Records Society, 1997), table 4. Marder reports that in October 1918, 257 British warships were directly engaged in convoy escort. Even if, as he suggests, another five hundred served as occasional escorts, the total of 757 would add up to only 25 percent of Britain's overall seagoing ASW effort. See Arthur J. Marder, *From the Dreadnought to Scapa Flow*, vol. 5, *1918–1919: Victory and Aftermath* (London: Oxford Univ. Press, 1970), p. 105.

37. National Archives, Kew, U.K., ADM 116/1809, *Private Correspondence of Sir Eric Geddes, First Lord of the Admiralty 1917–1919*, vol. 6, "Statement by Geddes to U.S. Press, October 13, 1918."

38. The Admiralty reported in May 1918 that about a half-million tons of shipping were lost annually due to irreparable war damage. See National Archives, Kew, U.K., ADM116/1807, *Private Correspondence of Sir Eric Geddes, First Lord of the Admiralty, 1917–1919*, vol. 4, "Report by Director of Statistics, Admiralty, May 21, 1918." Losses due to marine risk are reported in ADM167/153, Copy of Board Minute, *Meetings of the Board of Admiralty, August 1917 to December 1918*, "Admiralty Draft Memorandum to War Cabinet of 8 February, 1918."

39. National Archives, Kew, U.K., CAB23/3, *War Cabinet Papers, June 5th 1917 to August 30th 1917*, Minutes of August 2, 1917, Memorandum by Admiralty on "The Submarine Menace."

40. Cited in Schröder, *Die U-Boote des Kaisers*, p. 390.

41. Grove, *Defeat of the Enemy Attack on Shipping 1939–1945,* table 1.

42. Ibid., p. 10.

43. Marder, *1918–1919: Victory and Aftermath,* p. 103.

44. Sims, *Victory at Sea,* p. 135.

45. Ibid., p. 110.

46. Krause, *U-Boot Alarm,* p. 69.

47. See Patrick Beesly, *Room 40: British Naval Intelligence 1914–1918* (New York: Harcourt Brace Jovanovich, 1982), p. 260.

48. Cited in ibid.

49. Schröder, *Die U-Boote des Kaisers,* p. 372.

50. Ibid., p. 61.

51. Ibid., pp. 261–62.

52. Ibid., p. 261.

53. Sims, *Victory at Sea,* p. 130.

54. Cited in Robert M. Grant, *U-boat Intelligence 1914–1918* (Hamden, Conn.: Archon Books, 1969), p. 12.

55. Marder, *1918–1919: Victory and Aftermath,* p. 61.

56. Grant, *U-boat Intelligence 1914–1918,* p. 109.

57. S. W. Roskill, *The Strategy of Sea Power* (London: Collins, 1962), p. 135, cited in Marder, *1918–1919: Victory and Aftermath,* p. 76.

Conclusion

In his account of World War I, Churchill labeled the convoy decision "the decisive step" that defeated the U-boats. He even cites the escorts' successful "offensive actions."[1] Yet a world war later, when convoying again proved the salvation of allied shipping, he confided that "I always sought to rupture this defensive obsession by searching for forms of counteroffensive. . . . I could not rest content with the policy of 'convoy and blockade.'"[2] Together, the two pronouncements fairly sum up the continuing ambivalence among many senior naval officers on the subject of the convoy. By any logical and empirical measure, convoying had clearly shown itself to be the most, perhaps only, effective means of defeating the submarine's tonnage-sinking capacity. It worked, and everyone, even skeptics, agreed it did. Yet for many officers this was not enough—they simply did not *like* it. Which raises the question, of course: Why was the Admiralty so resistant to the convoy system to begin with? And when it proved its worth, why were the admirals quite ready to abandon it and concentrate resources instead on the fruitless hunt-and-kill method? This concluding section seeks to address these questions in the hope that the answers will shed further light on the nature of military innovation—or more precisely, on the nature of *resistance* to innovation, in this case *counter*-innovation.

One theory holds that Lloyd George's "High Admirals" were innately incapable of change, that among the world's admiralties, the British Admiralty took first place for hideboundness.[3] It is certainly true that navies generally, the Royal Navy in particular, have tended to be more traditionalist than sister services on land and in the air and have often been resistant to "interference," especially from the outside, in what they believe are their institutional core missions and capabilities. This said, though, the British navy and its leadership on the eve of World War I do not come across as more anti-innovation than other navies of the period. On the contrary, a fair argument can be made that the men who directed the Royal Navy in 1914–18 had been and still were on the cutting edge of technical innovation at the time. When Jellicoe took over as First Sea Lord in 1917, he had already been in the navy for forty-five years. During those years, his navy had changed from muzzle-loading to breech-loading guns; torpedoes, torpedo boats, and mines had joined the naval armories; wireless communications had became standard equipment; and of course, the submarine and aircraft had been introduced. The Royal Navy during the two decades or so leading up to World War I was

constantly testing and experimenting with new weapons, tactics, wireless communications, and even airborne "ocean surveillance."[4] In short, Jellicoe's navy was "thoroughly
modern."[5]

There are two caveats, though. First, the navy had little difficulty in accepting and
encouraging innovations that promised to improve what it saw as its "essential"
missions and capabilities. Those turned mainly on the efficiency of the *battle fleet*—
more accurate and longer-range firepower, improved radio signaling, and so forth. Less
likely to be embraced were innovations that did not obviously fit the institution's self-
image of an offensive battle force. An example is the Admiralty's rejection in 1902 of a
proposal to use captive balloons for submarine detection.[6] Submarines, let alone anti-
submarine measures, were far removed from the navy's "organizational essence" in
1902.[7] The second caveat is that the navy's willingness to experiment with and adopt
new technologies was largely limited to the *material* side of the fleet. Ever since the
industrial revolution at sea, when sailing fleets gave way to ironclads, the intellectual
milieu of the navy had been dominated by the "material school." Officers had become
preoccupied with technical developments, and what passed for "strategy" had been
images of war based on the (perceived) material possibilities of the fleet, not a careful
analysis of national needs and the threats to those needs.[8] In this mind-set there was little room for strategic or tactical innovativeness. The rare officer on the eve of World
War I who dared question the Admiralty's fixation on a dreadnought-style battle of
Trafalgar risked banishment to a distant and prospectless colonial cruiser station.[9]

Jellicoe was a dedicated materialist; he had specialized in gunnery, not strategic planning (which was not something in which officers could have specialized in any case).
He was dubbed the "granite sailor"—it is not clear why, but the name befits his reputa-
tion for stubbornness. Being stubborn in the face of adversity can be a positive asset,
but in Jellicoe's case it unfortunately also translated into an excessive loyalty to "the
plan" and a resistance to adaptation when circumstances changed.[10] The "plan" in 1914,
and still in 1917, was, first, to blockade Germany, and second, to keep the High Sea
Fleet in jail or, should it break out, send it to the bottom of the sea. It was, according to
one of Jellicoe's more sympathetic biographers, "the only basically sane strategy."[11] It
was also a "familiar" strategy; denying the enemy's trade and bottling up his fleet
through command of the sea had long been among the Royal Navy's tried and true
"principles." Convoying, on the other hand, was an unknown. No one knew whether it
would work, the risks of failure seemed substantial, and if stubbornness was one trait
of Jellicoe's, caution and averseness to risk were two others. He was temperamentally
suited to resist "eccentric pressures for change."[12]

The tendency to avoid decisions that involve risk (and change is risky by definition) is arguably the sine qua non of government bureaucracies. There is no evidence that the Admiralty was an exception—on the contrary. This suggests that an alternative, or possibly reinforcing, explanation for its long-delayed convoy decision is to be found in the organization's structure. Two aspects of the Admiralty in particular seem to have militated against a rapid and radical response to the U-boat threat. First, this was an extremely hierarchical organization, in which the discussion of naval strategic options was tightly concentrated at the very top, the Board of Admiralty. When Jellicoe joined the board in December 1916, it was being expanded from three to five senior admirals (the Sea Lords) and was presided over by a civilian cabinet minister, the First Lord, then Sir Edward Carson. With responsibility for operations, the First Sea Lord, in this case Jellicoe, was primus inter pares. Incredible as it sounds, the First Sea Lord, who headed the largest and most powerful fleet in the world and was responsible for the design and execution of its war plans, did not have a staff, properly speaking, until after the disastrous Dardanelles campaign. To be sure, a rudimentary staff, the Operations Division, headed up by a two-star Chief of the War Staff, had been in existence since shortly before the war, but only at the insistence of the then First Lord, Winston Churchill, and despite the protestations of his First Sea Lord, "Jackie" Fisher. Fisher's predecessor, Sir Arthur Wilson, had resigned rather than assist in bringing a naval staff into being.[13] Fisher made sure, though, that the Admiralty's new "Thinking Establishments" (Fisher's term) were kept at arm's length, noting with considerable glee after the war that only he and Admiral Wilson "knew the Naval plan of war."[14] It is no surprise that this first attempt at a staff did not attract many bright, career-minded officers.

After the report on the Dardanelles fiasco was published, the posts of First Sea Lord and Chief of the War Staff were merged. Also created in support of the new First Sea Lord qua Chief of Naval Staff (CNS) were the new posts of Assistant Chief of Naval Staff (ACNS) and Deputy Chief of Naval Staff (DCNS). Both were given seats on the board. In theory, this was an improvement, but in reality it was not until after World War I that the naval staff became a modern system worthy of the name.[15]

The Operations Division, which ostensibly served as Jellicoe's naval staff, numbered between two dozen and thirty officers.[16] As Captain DeWar recalled in his book, on paper this looked pretty imposing. Unfortunately, he wrote, none of the officers had had any staff training, their actual work had little to do with operations, and most were kept busy with menial tasks that, according to DeWar, could have been easily handled by clerks.

The preoccupation of experienced officers with minutiae pervaded the Admiralty right up to the top. Again according to DeWar, the men who were in charge of a global war at sea were commonly overwhelmed by petty tasks that could have been easily taken care of by local commanders.[17] Neither did it help that Jellicoe was by nature a micro-manager who, for example, would involve himself directly in the choice of the caliber of guns to be put on merchantmen. It is not particularly surprising, then, that a military organization whose senior leadership was preoccupied with the day-to-day business of the fleet and whose junior officers were discouraged from independent thinking found it difficult to look at the U-boats as a *strategic* and *analytical* problem.

There is a large body of organizational theory that is virtually unanimous in the opinion that hierarchical organizations are not likely incubators of innovation. If we are to believe John Sculley, chief executive officer and president of Apple Computers, "innovation has never coeme through bureaucracy and hierarchy. It's always come from individuals."[18] Sculley overstates the case; plenty of innovative success stories have emanated from extremely hierarchically structured organizations, including the military. But if a military hierarchy is to generate innovation, it must operate under at least these two conditions: first, the organization's leadership must limit its control to providing broad strategic guidance; and second, the leadership should encourage, indeed expect, subordinates to be flexible in translating this guidance into practical options. In short, the organization should be one that combines a high degree of centralized command over broad strategic goals with a *de*-centralized control over tactical and operational execution.

Closely related is the second condition, that the organization foster a strong pro-intellectual environment—that is to say, an environment in which the organization's members (in the case of the military, midgrade officers) are encouraged and rewarded for defining problems and advancing solutions that may not conform with agreed policy or doctrine. This also means that the organization must provide and value a strong analytical capability. There is a tendency still in military organizations to confuse analysis with "professional judgment," dismissing the former as overly academic and irrelevant to the "real world" of the military, while holding up the latter as common sense, embedded in sound military experience.

In truth, there is no inherent conflict between the two. In some circumstances, especially those with ample precedent, acting by the book and without further analysis may be quite adequate—but it usually is not. Analysis becomes absolutely mandatory, however, when the problem at hand is entirely novel and we cannot turn to experience, doctrine, or established policy for solutions-that-worked-in-the-past. Analysis is the basic tool of problem solving and innovation; without analysis we may not even be able to recognize the problem. An organization will not likely innovate if it is pervaded by anti-intellectualism and does not value analytical inquiry.

The British Admiralty of World War I was, to use Michael Simpson's phrase, a "creaking giant" that was organizationally incapable of visualizing the U-boat problem in other than the pre-U-boat tactical, or at best operational, terms.[19] A report by the American novelist Winston Churchill (no relation to the prime minister) to President Wilson on the state of the Admiralty was scathing on this score:

> I have become convinced that the criticism of the British Admiralty to the effect that it has been living from day to day, that it has been making no plans ahead, is justified. The several Sea Lords are of the conservative school, and they have been so encumbered by administrative and bureaucratic duties that they have found insufficient time to decide upon a future strategy. The younger and more imaginative element of that service has not been given a chance to show its powers, nor has it been consulted in matters of strategy. . . . [T]he Admiralty is still suffering from the inertia of a tradition that clings to the belief that the British navy still controls the seas, and can be made to move but slowly in new direction.[20]

This was an organization with a structure and culture that made failure to innovate against the submarine almost unavoidable. This was more than just a hierarchy topped by a handful of men who shared the same values and beliefs about the nature and "rules" of war at sea. That handicap could have been overcome if the Admiralty had been a "command hierarchy," in which the board provided and oversaw the overall strategic direction of the war but left the responsibility for operational and tactical planning with a war staff. But this was a "*control* hierarchy," run by leaders who had never managed to make the transition from the narrow tactical and operational expertness required of them when commanding ships or fleets to the broader outlook demanded of strategic leadership. These were micromanagers who insisted on retaining the tight tactical control they had been accustomed to on board their ships.[21] Differing ideas or alternative solutions by junior officers on the staff were neither encouraged nor welcomed; worse, those who persisted in questioning current policy risked disciplinary action. The junior officers who dared suggesting different ways of tackling the U-boats saw their opinions dismissed for their lack of experience (never mind that no one had ever fought an ASW campaign before). Even more objectionable were the ideas of "laymen"—civilians who, "because of the want of appreciation of the true relative size of the oceans and of the vessels on them . . . find difficulty in understanding the naval problems inherent in the protection of commerce."[22]

It is no wonder that between the board's preoccupation with tactical and material minutiae, the staff's reluctance to voice views contrary to Admiralty policy, and finally, the civilian leadership's habit of deference to the "experts," the big strategic picture was rarely contemplated. In any case, the capability to do strategic analysis, to set goals and evaluate alternative strategies, did not exist. Big decisions with large consequences were made in, to put it kindly, a kind of hit-and-miss fashion. The making of naval strategy and war plans, Admiral Fisher declared, was a straightforward business that called for common sense, not officers "attracted to the brainy work" of a naval staff.[23] There was no need for brains, or at least not brains attuned to thinking strategically, because, Fisher wrote, modern sea warfare had no secrets. It had become a "pure game of chess," whose outcome, thanks to autopropulsion and wireless, had become quite predictable. What need for analysis was there when the "Germans are just as capable as ourselves of planning out what is the best thing we can do?"[24]

Until the very end of the war, the Admiralty's staff organization was indeed little more than the "very excellent organization for cutting out and arranging foreign newspaper clippings" that Fisher had argued could and should be expected of it.[25] No wonder that, according to DeWar, no one planned, thought ahead, or investigated the relative merits and demerits of convoying or patrolling.[26] It was not encouraged, and in any case, the "facts" that would have made possible such a "cost-effectiveness analysis" did not exist, at least not at the Admiralty. Officers like Henderson and DeWar had to risk their careers and go to the Ministry of Shipping to find out the basic shipping data that would have allowed such a comparison. One Royal Navy officer, writing twenty years after the war, blamed the lack of a naval staff for the Admiralty's ignorance of the most basic shipping information. He wrote, "It cannot be regarded as other than remarkable that, whereas the protection of trade had always been accepted as a principal liability of the Navy, the prewar Navy had taken no steps to ascertain the exact extent of the liability. It is as if an insurance company agreed to insure a man's life without troubling to find out his age, occupation, or state of health."[27]

There may be yet another reason why the Admiralty did not collect and maintain current or reliable shipping statistics and yet did maintain minute supervision over the fleet's daily dispositions and routines: keeping track of merchant shipping was not seen as part of the navy's core business. This is comprehensible from an organizational perspective, for it has long been recognized that organizations tend to pay less attention to activities that are not considered essential to their basic missions. That is not the same as saying that the Royal Navy did not see defense of trade as an important responsibility. On the contrary, as the author just cited has remarked, safeguarding trade ranked, along with defense against invasion and protection of the empire, as a primary strategic responsibility. The problem was the navy's *operational* interpretation of the defense-of-trade strategic priority. Systemic handicaps—excessive centralization, a preoccupation with administrative and tactical detail, and a pervasive culture of anti-intellectualism— virtually precluded the Admiralty's effectiveness as an innovating institution. But overarching all these factors was a more deep-seated problem, namely, the tendency to see the protection of shipping and the sinking of U-boats as separate and distinct operational problems rather than two parts of a single strategic dilemma. This confusion helps explain Churchill's frustration with the (operationally) "defensive" nature of the convoy system despite its *strategic* success. It also helps explain why, even as evidence of the convoy's success steadily accumulated, naval planners refused to acknowledge the failure of the hunting method and repeatedly pleaded that escorts be directed from their "defensive" tasks to "offensive" operations.

Two commentaries by the Admiralty's First Lord, Sir Eric Geddes, are revealing in this regard. The first was made during an allied naval conference in Rome in February 1918, in response to the question of an Italian admiral, Paolo Thaon Di Revel, regarding whether it was "better to harass and attack the submarines in coming out [of the Straits of Otranto], or is it better to defend convoys by means of escorts?" The First Lord replied it had been the experience so far in both the North Atlantic and North Sea that the convoy escorts had

> in fact destroyed very few submarines. . . . It is not the escort forces which are really getting the number of submarines, and while we would be the last to reduce escorts if we could destroy the submarines by their means, we feel that to go on with a purely defensive measure is an unsuccessful policy. . . . Very few submarines have been destroyed [in the Mediterranean and Adriatic], and the only way to deal with the submarine menace is to go from the purely escorting side of the organiza-tion on to an offensive organization.[28]

Geddes's second comment came in a memorandum on a conference with high-level U.S. Navy officials in Washington, D.C. Note that the date was 8 October 1918; by this time the German war effort was collapsing. The memorandum itself said the following: "It had long been realized that defensive measures and offensive-defensive measures, such as the convoy system, although affording a great measure of safety to the mercan-tile marine and resulting in the destruction of some submarines, were quite inadequate by themselves to counter the submarine menace."[29] The paper went on to recommend a resumption of hunting tactics as soon as more forces became available. The Admiralty's reasoning behind the memorandum makes for even more interesting reading. In "Notes for Guidance as to the Line to Be Adopted" with the Americans, the "diversion" of Royal Navy warships from hunt-and-kill to escorting U.S. troopships was blamed for what the Admiralty claimed to be a worsening U-boat picture. The Admiralty's "line" included these highlights:

> The demands for safeguarding American seaborne traffic . . . have become . . . from a purely Naval point of view . . . a tax on the Alliance [that] has entirely fallen upon the British with the result that we have had to utilize essential forces intended for hunting the submarine. . . . Up to May of this year submarines were being satisfactorily dealt with. Since May, mainly on account of the diversion of the British hunting forces to American escort work, the submarine situation has steadily become more formidable, and we are now faced with a tremendous submarine effort on the enemy's part whilst our hunting forces are inadequate for the reasons given. . . . During the last quarter of 1917 and the first quarter of 1918, the British Navy was able . . . effectively to hold the submarine menace, and there is every reason to believe that the destruction of submarines would have continued had the demand for defensive escort not been so vast and imperative. *The anti-submarine campaign for 1918 in a great measure had to be, and was, abandoned* and we must now look to 1919 and lay our plans.[30]

Specialists in Naval Victory

The complaint that the demand for escorts had forced the abandonment of the battle against the U-boats is starkly revealing of the narrow, tactics- and operations-focused mind-set of the naval leadership at the time. The officers who led and manned the Royal Navy in 1914–18 were what Barry Posen has called "specialists in victory."[31] More precisely, they were specialists in *naval* victory. Military organizations, according to Posen, prefer offensive doctrines, for a variety of reasons. For one, it is a long-standing "principle of war" that only by attacking the enemy can he be defeated. Defensive doctrines, in contrast, have rarely found favor among modern militaries. As Posen puts it, they are seen as turning soldiers (and sailors) into "specialists in attrition."[32] For the naval leadership in World War I, victory meant seeking out and defeating the enemy fleet. This was so at all levels of warfare—strategic, operational, and tactical. The ideal victory was to be won by defeating the enemy fleet in a decisive battle. Should the enemy refuse to come out and fight, he was to be bottled up in his ports and harbors. Either way, the "victor" could now enjoy all the benefits of command of the sea: the country was secure from invasion, overseas possessions were safe, and friendly ships could ply the seas without fear of enemy interference. In short, defeating the enemy fleet promised to fulfill for the Royal Navy, in one operational stroke, every one of its strategic responsibilities. Defeating the enemy's war-making capacity at sea was, therefore, the *navy's* way of protecting trade.

The various methods employed by the British to cope with the U-boats reflected this narrow operational perspective. Without a "traditional" enemy fleet to hunt down and send to the bottom of the sea, the hunting patrols, though largely fruitless, were a facsimile of the "close engagement" and captured its spirit. Success (or its lack) was measured by the number of U-boats killed. It was thanks to the *offensive* measures introduced by Jellicoe, as Bacon wrote of his former commander in chief, that the submarine menace had been "practically conquered" by the end of 1917: "We were sinking submarines at the same rate as they were being produced in Germany."[33] Declines in merchant ship losses were usually attributed to the success of offensive measures, whereas increased losses were typically blamed on changes in U-boat tactics or weaponry, not failure by the fleet to reassess its own tactics, let alone strategic vision. The admirals never managed to escape from the narrow, presubmarine operational paradigm that dominated their "specialization," that ASW—that is to say, sinking U-boats—and protecting shipping were two different, even competing, tasks. It took "nonspecialists"—civilians and junior officers not burdened by the legacy of Trafalgar—to elevate the problem of defeating the submarine from the tactical-operational domain to the strategic level of war. The convoy system shifted the focus of countermeasures away from defeating the U-boat to defeating the U-boat's war-making *purposes*.

DEFEATING THE U-BOAT   77

Professor Marder put it best when he wrote that this entirely different, even revolutionary, way of looking at the problem meant that "sinking submarines is a bonus, not a necessity."[34]

The story of the invention of the submarine and the subsequent struggle to defeat its revolutionary war-making power has a wide range of possible implications, "lessons" if you will, for the "transformation" of the American military today. For one, the use of the submarine for commerce raiding rather than "legitimate" naval warfare against grey hulls is a reminder that radical military innovations may be used for purposes and in ways neither planned nor anticipated by their originators. The struggle to find a solution to the U-boat problem of 1914–18 is also a reminder that truly revolutionary military innovations, because they *are* revolutionary, are extremely difficult to defeat using "legacy" techniques at the tactical and operational levels of war. The U-boat in both world wars was never defeated at the force-on-force, tactical level. Its defeat became possible only when the problem was revisualized as a *strategic* issue and it was realized that victory or failure hinged on the preservation of shipping and cargoes, not "hull counts" of submarines sunk. Redefining the problem from the tactical to strategic level of analysis is central to the idea of asymmetric warfare. A clever future opponent should therefore be expected to counter a high-tech U.S. military by striking against its *strategic* vulnerabilities.

Finally and perhaps most obviously, one of the most difficult things for military organizations to overcome is their tendency to think of problems and search for solutions within a strategic framework, setting aside the operational culture that defines their organizational essence. The Royal Navy was in the years before World War I the most successful navy in memory; its war-fighting culture was naturally centered on the idea of the offensive. Its perception of its role and responsibility in the next war was a narrow, operational one—seek out the enemy fleet and sink it; any suggestion that *national* interests, such as the protection of trade, might demand a broader perspective was dismissed as "interference" in the business the navy knew best. This outlook, in which success was measured in narrow *naval* terms—enemy ships sunk—when combined with the Admiralty leadership's proclivity to micromanage the fleet's daily tactical and administrative routines, was bound to produce a culture resistant to change.

Organizational theory proposes that large organizations, especially military ones, tend to resist tasks and missions that they do not see as part of their cultures. But there is one exception: an organization will embrace new responsibilities, reluctantly perhaps, when its survival or legitimacy is at stake. The Royal Navy's legitimacy was in question in 1917. The British army had been doing almost all the dying on the western front, while, in the public eye at least, the navy merely "watched and waited" for the High Sea

Fleet to sortie and present the opportunity to fight a decisive North Sea Trafalgar. The High Sea Fleet did make its appearance at the end of May 1916, but the outcome was hardly what the navy's propagandists had led the British public to expect. Yet, even the navy's failure in what it had always insisted was its very raison d'être did not stimulate a wholesale strategic reassessment of the *real* war it was, or at least *should* have been, fighting. It took the circumvention of the navy's formal hierarchy by a few relatively junior officers to make the political leadership aware that the navy's rejection of the convoy system had been based in good part on an inflated estimate of the magnitude of the task. When Lloyd George had the "real" numbers and knew that far fewer resources were needed than the navy had maintained, he could confidently override the professionals' judgment.

Notes

1. Winston S. Churchill, *The World Crisis 1911–1918* (London: Odhams, 1923–27), vol. 2, pp. 1233, 1235. Churchill also pointed out that it was he, as First Lord of the Admiralty, who instituted the troopship convoys at the beginning of the war.

2. Winston S. Churchill, *The Second World War,* vol. 1, *The Gathering Storm* (London: Cassell, 1948), pp. 262–63.

3. According to one author, speaking with particular reference to the Royal Navy, "In every major nation the Navy was the most hidebound of the military services, perhaps due to the habitual isolation of ships at sea from the dictates of land-based supervisors or being the service most encumbered by tradition." Tom Shachtman, *Terrors and Marvels: How Science and Technology Changed the Character and Outcome of World War II* (New York: William Morrow, 2002), p. 28.

4. Possibly the earliest experiment in airborne surveillance of the sea surface took place in 1902, involving a camera-equipped balloon flight by the Reverend J. M. Bacon across the Irish Channel. The clergyman had asked the Admiralty to "grant me the attendance of some vessel in case of immersion." The Navy complied, the flight was successful, and at least two photographs were taken, proving that the bottom of the ocean could be photographed from high altitude. National Archives, Kew, U.K., ADM116/652, "Balloon Experiments," Rev. J. M. Bacon in 9 November 1902 letter to the Admiralty regarding his planned Irish Channel balloon flight. That same year, Bacon published his classic *The Dominion of the Air: The Story of Aerial Navigation.*

5. Donald M. Schurman, "Admiral Sir John Jellicoe (1916–1917)," in *The First Sea Lords: From Fisher to Mountbatten,* ed. Malcolm H. Murfett (Westport, Conn.: Praeger, 1995), p. 101.

6. The proposal and the Admiralty's response are reported in *The Dominion of the Air: The Story of Aerial Navigation,* available at www.worldwideschool.org/.

7. Morton H. Halperin and his co-authors defined "organizational essence" as the view held by the dominant group in an organization of what the roles and capabilities of the organization should be. See his *Bureaucratic Politics and Foreign Policy* (Washington, D.C.: Brookings Institution, 1974), p. 28.

8. See Commodore Daniel McNeil, "Technology, History and the Revolution in Military Affairs," *Canadian Military Journal* (Winter 2000–2001).

9. Captain, later Admiral, Sir Herbert Richmond was one of the few intellectual dissenters—or, as he called himself and others like him, "heretics." After a plum command of HMS *Dreadnought,* his unsolicited strategic advice was rewarded with command of two second-class cruisers. Ibid., p. 10.

10. One severe critic wrote of Jellicoe that "it took him time to receive the good message and longer still to deliver it." Stanley Bonnett, *The Price of Admiralty: An Indictment of the Royal Navy 1805–1966* (London: Robert Hale, 1968), p. 204.

11. Schurman, "Admiral Sir John Jellicoe (1916–1917)," p. 108.

12. Ibid., p. 190.

13. Cdr. Russell Grenfell, *The Art of the Admiral* (London: Faber and Faber, 1937), p. 87.

14. Admiral of the Fleet Lord Fisher, *Memories* (London: Hodder and Stoughton, 1919), p. 102.

15. Malcolm H. Murfett, "The First Sea Lords (1904–1950): An Overview," in *The First Sea Lords*, ed. Murfett, p. 1.

16. Captain DeWar reports a staff of about two dozen officers and a couple of civilian assistants; Vice Adm. K. G. B. DeWar, *The Navy from Within* (London: Victor Gollancz, 1939), p. 215. Another contemporary account claims that the Admiralty's "strategical staff" involved about thirty officers. Winston Churchill, "Naval Organization, American and British," *Atlantic* (August 1917). The author is not to be confused with Winston Spencer Churchill, Britain's prime minister during World War II; this Winston Churchill (1871–1947) was an American novelist, who had the ear of President Wilson. While in London as an "independent observer," he wrote Wilson a number of critical reports on the British Admiralty.

17. DeWar, *Navy from Within*, p. 227.

18. *Schipul: The Web Marketing Company*, www.schipul.com/.

19. Michael Simpson, ed., *Anglo-American Naval Relations 1917–1919* (Aldershot, U.K.: Gower for the Navy Records Society, 1991), p. 59.

20. Winston Churchill to President Wilson, 22 October 1917, cited in ibid., pp. 118–19.

21. As Marder has reported, the German naval high command operated under a very different philosophy. It defined overall strategic policy for each subsidiary command in brief "war orders"; beyond intelligence reports and occasional directives, it did not issue operational orders; Arthur J. Marder, *From the Dreadnought to Scapa Flow*, vol. 5, *1918–1919: Victory and Aftermath* (London:

Oxford Univ. Press, 1970), p. 329. The same contrast was true between the British and German armies.

22. Adm. Sir R. H. Bacon, *The Life of John Rushworth Earl Jellicoe* (London: Cassell, 1936), p. 349.

23. Fisher, *Memories*, p. 109.

24. National Archives, Kew, U.K., ADM116/1043B, "War Plans & the Distribution of the Fleet."

25. Fisher, *Memories*, p. 108.

26. Cited in Marder, *1918–1919: Victory and Aftermath*, p. 328.

27. Grenfell, *Art of the Admiral*, p. 87.

28. National Archives, Kew, U.K., ADM116/1807, *Private Correspondence of Sir Eric Geddes, 1917–1919*, vol. 4, "Report on Third Session of Allied Naval Conference, February 8&9, 1918."

29. National Archives, Kew, U.K., ADM116/1809, *Private Correspondence of Sir Eric Geddes, 1917–1919*, vol. 6, "Memorandum of a Conference Held at the Navy Department on 8th October, 1918 to Discuss the Naval Situation."

30. National Archives, Kew, U.K., ADM 116/1809, *Private Correspondence of Sir Eric Geddes, First Lord of the Admiralty 1917–1919*, vol. 6, "Notes for Guidance as to the Line to Be Adopted in Conference with U.S. Navy Department and in Informal Discussions," undated [emphasis added].

31. Barry R. Posen, *The Sources of Military Doctrine: France, Britain, and Germany between the World Wars* (Ithaca, N.Y.: Cornell Univ. Press, 1984), p. 50.

32. Ibid.

33. Bacon, *Life of John Rushworth Earl Jellicoe*, p. 371. Bacon was basically correct in his assertion that toward the end of 1917 about as many U-boats were being sunk as came off the slipways. Twenty-two boats were lost in the last quarter of that year, compared with twenty-four added; Joachim Schröder, *Die U-Boote des Kaisers* (Bonn: Bernard and Graefe Verlag, 2003), p. 437. Bacon did not mention that most sinkings were the work of "defensive" escorts.

34. Marder, *1918–1919: Victory and Aftermath*, p. 103 [emphasis in the original].

Abbreviations

A **ACNS**   Assistant Chief of Naval Staff

   AEF   American Expeditionary Force

   ASW   antisubmarine warfare

B **BIR**   Board of Invention and Research

C **CNS**   Chief of Naval Staff

D **DCNS**   Deputy Chief of Naval Staff

   DER   Department of Experiments and Research

About the Author

Dr. Breemer is a professor of National Security Decision Making at the Naval War College's Monterey Program, in Monterey, California. He earned his PhD in international relations at the University of Southern California, Los Angeles. After a twelve-year stint as a professional defense analyst in the Washington, D.C., area, he joined the Department of National Security Affairs of the Naval Postgraduate School in Monterey. In 1992, he was appointed a Senior Secretary of the Navy Research Fellow at the Naval War College, Newport, Rhode Island; eight years later, he joined the Naval War College faculty in Monterey. Dr. Breemer is the author of *U.S. Naval Developments* (Nautical and Aviation, 1983) and *Soviet Submarines: Design, Development, and Tactics* (Jane's Information Group, 1989), as well as of numerous journal articles and chapters in edited collections. He is currently preparing a book manuscript reexamining the importance of radar in the Battle of Britain.

The Newport Papers

Piracy and Maritime Crime: Historical and Modern Case Studies, edited by Bruce A. Elleman, Andrew Forbes, and David Rosenberg (no. 35, January 2010).

Somalia . . . From the Sea, by Gary Ohls (no. 34, July 2009).

U.S. Naval Strategy in the 1980s: Selected Documents, edited by John B. Hattendorf and Peter M. Swartz (no. 33, December 2008).

Major Naval Operations, by Milan Vego (no. 32, September 2008).

Perspectives on Maritime Strategy: Essays from the Americas, edited by Paul D. Taylor (no. 31, August 2008).

U.S. Naval Strategy in the 1970s: Selected Documents, edited by John B. Hattendorf (no. 30, September 2007).

Shaping the Security Environment, edited by Derek S. Reveron (no. 29, September 2007).

Waves of Hope: The U.S. Navy's Response to the Tsunami in Northern Indonesia, by Bruce A. Elleman (no. 28, February 2007).

U.S. Naval Strategy in the 1990s: Selected Documents, edited by John B. Hattendorf (no. 27, September 2006).

Reposturing the Force: U.S. Overseas Presence in the Twenty-first Century, edited by Carnes Lord (no. 26, February 2006).

The Regulation of International Coercion: Legal Authorities and Political Constraints, by James P. Terry (no. 25, October 2005).

Naval Power in the Twenty-first Century: A Naval War College Review *Reader,* edited by Peter Dombrowski (no. 24, July 2005).

The Atlantic Crises: Britain, Europe, and Parting from the United States, by William Hopkinson (no. 23, May 2005).

China's Nuclear Force Modernization, edited by Lyle J. Goldstein with Andrew S. Erickson (no. 22, April 2005).

Latin American Security Challenges: A Collaborative Inquiry from North and South, edited by Paul D. Taylor (no. 21, 2004).

Global War Game: Second Series, 1984–1988, by Robert Gile (no. 20, 2004).

The Evolution of the U.S. Navy's Maritime Strategy, 1977–1986, by John Hattendorf (no. 19, 2004).

Military Transformation and the Defense Industry after Next: The Defense Industrial Implications of Network-Centric Warfare, by Peter J. Dombrowski, Eugene Gholz, and Andrew L. Ross (no. 18, 2003).

The Limits of Transformation: Officer Attitudes toward the Revolution in Military Affairs, by Thomas G. Mahnken and James R. FitzSimonds (no. 17, 2003).

The Third Battle: Innovation in the U.S. Navy's Silent Cold War Struggle with Soviet Submarines, by Owen R. Cote, Jr. (no. 16, 2003).

International Law and Naval War: The Effect of Marine Safety and Pollution Conventions during International Armed Conflict, by Dr. Sonja Ann Jozef Boelaert-Suominen (no. 15, December 2000).

Theater Ballistic Missile Defense from the Sea: Issues for the Maritime Component Commander, by Commander Charles C. Swicker, U.S. Navy (no. 14, August 1998).

Sailing New Seas, by Admiral J. Paul Reason, U.S. Navy, with David G. Freymann (no. 13, March 1998).

What Color Helmet? Reforming Security Council Peacekeeping Mandates, by Myron H. Nordquist (no. 12, August 1997).

The International Legal Ramifications of United States Counter-Proliferation Strategy: Problems and Prospects, by Frank Gibson Goldman (no. 11, April 1997).

Chaos Theory: The Essentials for Military Applications, by Major Glenn E. James, U.S. Air Force (no. 10, October 1996).

A Doctrine Reader: The Navies of the United States, Great Britain, France, Italy, and Spain, by James J. Tritten and Vice Admiral Luigi Donolo, Italian Navy (Retired) (no. 9, December 1995).

Physics and Metaphysics of Deterrence: The British Approach, by Myron A. Greenberg (no. 8, December 1994).

Mission in the East: The Building of an Army in a Democracy in the New German States, by Colonel Mark E. Victorson, U.S. Army (no. 7, June 1994).

The Burden of Trafalgar: Decisive Battle and Naval Strategic Expectations on the Eve of the First World War, by Jan S. Breemer (no. 6, October 1993).

Beyond Mahan: A Proposal for a U.S. Naval Strategy in the Twenty-First Century, by Colonel Gary W. Anderson, U.S. Marine Corps (no. 5, August 1993).

Global War Game: The First Five Years, by Bud Hay and Bob Gile (no. 4, June 1993).

The "New" Law of the Sea and the Law of Armed Conflict at Sea, by Horace B. Robertson, Jr. (no. 3, October 1992).

Toward a Pax Universalis: A Historical Critique of the National Military Strategy for the 1990s, by Lieutenant Colonel Gary W. Anderson, U.S. Marine Corps (no. 2, April 1992).

"Are We Beasts?" Churchill and the Moral Question of World War II "Area Bombing," by Christopher C. Harmon (no. 1, December 1991).

Newport Papers are available online (Acrobat required) at www.usnwc.edu/press/.